HOW TO HAVE A
FABULOUS,
ROMANTIC
HONEY-
MOON
ON A
BUDGET

DIANE WARNER

BETTERWAY BOOKS
CINCINNATI, OHIO

How to Have a Fabulous, Romantic Honeymoon on a Budget. Copyright ©
1993 by Diane Warner. Printed and bound in the United States of America. All rights
reserved. No part of this book may be reproduced in any form or by any electronic
or mechanical means including information storage and retrieval systems without
permission in writing from the publisher, except by a reviewer, who may quote
brief passages in a review. Published by Betterway Books, an imprint of F&W Publications, Inc., 1507 Dana Avenue, Cincinnati, Ohio 45207. 1-800-289-0963. First
edition.

97 96 95 94 93   5 4 3 2 1

Library of Congress Cataloging-in-Publication Data

Warner, Diane
    How to have a fabulous, romantic honeymoon on a budget / By Diane Warner.
      p.   cm.
    Includes index.
    ISBN 1-55870-317-9
    1. Honeymoon—United States. 2. Travel. I. Title.
GT2798.W37 1993
917.04'539—dc20   93-22157
                                                       CIP

Note: Due to the constantly changing nature of the travel industry, neither the
author nor the publisher make any guarantees as to availability or costs of features
described in this book.

Edited by Mark Garvey
Designed by Sandy Conopeotis

DEDICATION

With love to my husband, Jack

ACKNOWLEDGEMENTS

I want to thank all the honeymooners who contributed to the content of this book by sharing their "finds" and budget travel secrets.

Thanks to all the travel professionals who offered helpful advice to my readers and extra special thanks to Shirlene Hill and Terry Avalos, travel advisors at the California State Automobile Association office in Turlock, California. I also appreciate the help of the bureaus of tourism all around the country.

TABLE OF CONTENTS

INTRODUCTION

THE BASICS OF AFFORDABLE HONEYMOON PLANNING

A ROMANTIC HONEYMOON IN YOUR OWN HOME STATE

GREAT ESCAPES ON A BUDGET

SERENDIPITY HONEYMOONS

NOW IT'S ALL UP TO YOU

INTRODUCTION

So, you're getting married! Congratulations! And, like all new-lyweds, you want a fabulous, romantic honeymoon. After all the stress of planning and paying for a wedding, you deserve a great week or two together, some place special where you can relax, have fun, and enjoy your new roles as husband and wife.

Some newlyweds dream of a European-style bed-and-breakfast inn hidden in some bashful village. Others long for excitement and smashing entertainment, while most equate a romantic honeymoon with a hot, white-sand beach.

You can realize any of these dreams and more, all on affordable budgets of $200 to $1,500. Yes, there's a honeymoon that's perfect for your pocketbook; all you need to know are a few little tricks of the travel industry and the locations of all those romantic, affordable spots.

Read on, and enjoy!

THE BASICS OF AFFORDABLE HONEY~MOON PLANNING

CHAPTER 1

THE GREAT TREASURE HUNT
You <u>Can</u> Find a Honeymoon That Fits Your Budget

There are newlyweds all over the country who have had fabulous honeymoons on small budgets, and you can have one, too. This book will be your treasure map as you hunt for the *X* that marks your special honeymoon spot. However, this "treasure hunt" won't be like any you've ever been on before. You see, I've already dug up the bargains; I've even drawn your map and given you the clues. All you need to do is follow the trail that sounds good to you, read the clues, and stop at the *X* to pick up your treasure. It is there waiting for you.

What a fun time I had putting these clues together, and how happy I am that you really can have a fabulous, romantic honeymoon on a budget, just like this book title says. The more I researched, in fact, the more excited I became, for I realized that most newlyweds haven't traveled a whole lot and may not know the cost-cutting tricks of the travel industry, nor the affordable destinations, from their own state to Hawaii and the Caribbean.

To start off your treasure hunt, this is your most important clue:

It's who you're with, not how much you spend.

Most couples have been brainwashed into believing that it isn't a "real" honeymoon unless you fly off to some exotic spot or stay at an elegant couples-only honeymoon resort. Fortunately, this is a myth. When two people are deeply in love, every meal is a special meal; every walk is a special walk; and every honeymoon night is a special memory. The meal may be only a $5 picnic in the park; the walk may be only a hike along a public beach; and the honeymoon night may be spent in only a humble cottage.

Just remember this: More isn't always better. Don't feel that the more you spend the better your trip will be, because, as you read this book, you will see that what you really want are romantic memories, and often they come for free.

To give you an idea of what I mean, let me dribble a few clues for your treasure hunt. Let's start with a very small honeymoon budget and see what you can get for the money.

HONEYMOON BUDGETS OF $200 TO $300

Here is a true story of a couple who had a week-long honeymoon for about $200. The bride's uncle loaned them his pickup and camper, and they used it to sightsee, ending up in a secluded campground beside a high mountain lake. Now, here is the question: "Are two sleeping bags zipped together as romantic as a motel bed?" Of course they are! This couple can't stop talking about their honeymoon memories, from the raindrops that pinged against the roof of the camper, to the smell of bacon frying over an open campfire, to the six rainbow trout they caught in the lake. Their total honeymoon expense was ridiculously low, thanks to her uncle's generosity, but even if they had rented a camping trailer for a whole week, their expense still would have been under $400.

Other ways to hold your expenses under $300 are to honeymoon in your own home state (chapters 8 through 19), take a side trip down into Baja California, Mexico (chapter 22), spend a weekend in Canada (chapter 21), or take a "sporting vacation," much like the one described above (see chapters 25 and 28). Of course, the practicality of these ideas depends on where you live.

If you take a honeymoon in your own home state, which is the most likely possibility on a very small budget, you will need to use the affordable lodging ideas in chapter 2, such as doing a home exchange or finding a bargain bed-and-breakfast inn or motel. Then you will need to "eat cheap" by taking romantic picnics to the beach or park, eating off the appetizer menu, enjoying the free breakfast included in the room rate, or by "filling up for free" at a one-drink minimum happy-hour buffet. And of course, there are always the fast food restaurants.

You can be entertained for free by taking advantage of the dozens of ideas in chapter 6, "Freeloading Fun." There are free festivals, museums, tours, concerts, sports events, and gobs of sightseeing and people-watching attractions; you just need the "clues" so you can search them out. Your days can be filled with "go-see-do," all for the cost of a couple of ice cream cones!

Each state's suggested honeymoon destinations include free and low-cost attractions, as well.

HONEYMOON BUDGETS OF $300 TO $600

Use the same destination ideas I just gave you, but with the additional $300, stay longer and include a few special splurges. Each state's honeymoon destinations include ideas for "special splurges," such as an $18 round-trip on the Skunk Railroad, if you happen to be honeymooning on the Mendocino coast of northern California, or if you're in the Newport, Rhode Island, area, a special splurge might be the $13 Sunday brunch and jazz concert at an inn overlooking Narragansett Bay. You see how it works? With this additional cash, you can create some extra special honeymoon memories.

HONEYMOON BUDGETS OF $600 TO $900

In addition to honeymoons in your home state, Canadian honeymoons, sporting honeymoons, or a side trip into Mexico, a $900 budget will add these possible destinations:

A complete air package trip to Mexico (chapter 22).

A Caribbean cruise (chapter 24).

A couples-only honeymoon resort package (chapter 26).

An "exciting city" honeymoon (chapter 27).

Whether you can afford one of these destinations will depend on where you live. For example, a Mexican package for under $900 will probably require a flight out of Los Angeles; a three-day Caribbean cruise, starting at about $445 per person, will mean departure from Miami; an "exciting city" honeymoon will depend on your proximity to one of the five cities featured in that chapter; and a honeymoon resort destination will be possible only if you can drive there without a lot of expense.

It's amazing, though, what $900 can do by adding a few exotic possibilities.

HONEYMOON BUDGETS OF $900 TO $1,500

Now, we're talking the "big bucks"! With this amount of money you can select any treasure found on any page of this book, including Hawaii. Yes, even though a recent *Bride's* magazine survey said that the average Hawaiian honeymoon costs $4,500, there's a way you can do it for just $1,500. It means you can only visit Oahu, but, as you read the Hawaii chapter, you'll see that Oahu provides all the Polynesian thrills you can handle. Read chapter 20.

Are you ready for your treasure hunt? Are you excited? Good! I'm excited for you. Now, turn the page for your first set of clues.

CHAPTER 2

You Gotta Sleep Sometime
Affordable Honeymoon Accommodations

Your honeymoon abode—that's a pretty special treasure. In this chapter you will find ways to cut costs on your accommodations, ideas to be used if you make your own "à la carte" arrangements. Later in this book I will present dozens of package plans that include your accommodations, such as cruises, honeymoon destination resorts, guest ranches and a variety of air and land deals for Hawaii and Mexico, but in this chapter we will take a look at general advice that can be helpful to honeymooners. There are many affordable, romantic options out there for you to consider.

The Bed-and-Breakfast Hideaway—$50 to $125

A bed-and-breakfast inn is usually a small establishment offering a sensual atmosphere, along with special attention to guests' enjoyment. Rates are often less expensive than more "businesslike" accommodations, such as hotels, with even lower rates during the off-season or at midweek. You will want to avoid those establishments that have shared bath facilities, obviously unacceptable for honeymooners. Fortunately, most bed-and-breakfasts have private baths.

This type of accommodation usually has a schmaltzy name, such as The Feather Bed, Thistle Dew Inn or Cinnamon Bear Bed-and-Breakfast. Costs run an average of $75 for two people in one bed and usually include many of these amenities:

- Gourmet-quality breakfasts (available in your room).
- Complimentary cheese and wine reception.
- Hot tub and/or pool.
- Fireplace.
- Victorian decor.
- Private courtyard and room entrance.
- Antiques.
- Fresh-cut flowers at your bedside daily.
- Tea, coffee and homemade cookies available all day.
- Terry cloth robes.
- Daily newspapers.
- Feather beds.

- Whirlpool baths.
- Canopy beds and down comforters.
- Rooms with their own names, such as the Candlelight Suite, the Winemaker or the Champagne.

Speaking of "schmaltzy," here are some of the expressions used in their advertisements:

"Stargaze on the porch swing," "Cascading waterfalls, meandering brooks, romantic gazebo," "An envelope of comfort," "Each room a visual feast," "Away from the real world," "Lawn chairs under giant oak trees," "Mythical sleepy hollow by the sea," "Romance reminiscent of another era," "An island floating above the trees."

Schmaltzy or not, you have to admit that bed-and-breakfasts have romantic honeymoon appeal.

How can you find bed-and-breakfasts at your honeymoon destination? Just check the yellow pages under Bed & Breakfasts, or contact the local chambers of commerce. If you are a member of AAA (American Automobile Association), they will give you a free directory of bed-and-breakfast inns, otherwise, you need to look for *Frommer's Bed & Breakfast North America*, the most comprehensive directory for each state.

Affordable Hotels and Motels – $39 to $125

Contrast the bed-and-breakfast ads to these:

"Indoor pool . . . exercise room . . . coin laundry . . . pay valet garage . . . radios . . . phones . . . easy freeway access . . . adjacent to convention center . . ."

These ads aren't exactly enveloped in sensuality, yet many couples want the excitement of staying at a hotel or motel. To get their best rates, by the way, always call the hotel or motel directly; don't use their nationwide "800" numbers because the clerks at central registration are told to quote the highest rates. The only way to get this rate down is to ask questions. In fact, one hotel manager confided that the caller who gets the lowest price is the one who asks the most questions. Also, individual hotels and motels have more leeway with pricing than do the "800" clerks. If you would like to call the national reservation's number to check for availability, however, I have included a complete list under Resources at the end of this book.

The general appeal of a large hotel or motel seems to be in their anonymity, especially compared to a small bed-and-breakfast inn. Honeymooners also like the choice of fine restaurants, entertainment, glamorous lobbies, high-rise views, elevators and the room amenities, especially those found in the honeymoon suite. If this type of accommodation appeals to you, there are a few ways to have the nicest room possible for the least cost. Consider the suggestions that follow.

- ASK FOR THEIR HONEYMOON SPECIAL.
  Most of the larger hotel chains, and many of the smaller hotels and motels, have a special package deal for honeymooners. Whenever you're calling around for the best deal, be sure to ask about their honeymoon packages. Here is a typical package, offered by the Hilton Hotels, called Hilton's Wedding Night Romance Package:
  Up-graded room accommodations
  Chilled champagne awaiting your arrival
  Full American breakfast, served in your room
  Pre-registration, for easy check-in
  Late check-out privileges
  Free use of health spa, pool and whirlpool spa
  There is an all-inclusive price for this package that varies for different cities, but seems to range from $100 to $125. Call (800)HILTONS for prices at your honeymoon destination.
- SAVE WITH A PACKAGE TOUR.
  Purchase your hotel stay as part of a package tour. This is always cheaper than arranging for everything separately. This is especially true in Hawaii, which we will cover in chapter 20.
- BENEFIT FROM OFF-SEASON BOOKING.
  Book your hotel room for up to 75 percent off during off-season. Be aware that the term "off-season" is determined solely by the hotel itself; in fact, hotels in the same city often have different off-season dates. Here is a sampling of off-seasons for various destinations:

Aspen, Colorado	April through November
Las Vegas, Nevada	June through September
Miami, Florida	May through September
Hawaii	October and November
The Virgin Islands	April through September

  Smart honeymooners schedule their weddings within a couple of weeks of either end of the off-season. This way they can enjoy the much reduced off-season prices while the weather is still tolerable.
- JOIN A HOTEL DISCOUNT CLUB.
  If you join a discount club ahead of time at a cost of $30 to $100, you will receive 50 percent off on most hotel and motel rooms. There are a few restrictions, however; for example, the discount usually doesn't apply to the least expensive room, and the dis-

count may only be available on a space available basis, but the savings are worth it. My husband and I have belonged to Entertainment Publications and Quest International for years and have found them to be as advertised. Every time we visit the San Francisco Bay area, we stay in the nicest room at the Howard Johnson's resort at a discount price of only $44 per night. There are a variety of clubs to consider. Give them a call; their names and numbers are listed on pages 176-177 of Resources. Ask for their brochures or get information over the telephone.

- LOOK FOR SPECIAL HOTEL RATES.

Many big-city hotels that cater to the weekday business traveler entice vacationers with special weekend rates. Many times the weekend rate includes a two-night stay (Friday and Saturday evenings), one meal, a show ticket, afternoon cheese and wine tasting, free valet parking or airport shuttle, and the daily newspaper—all for 50 to 60 percent off their regular rate. Likewise, hotels that cater to weekend vacationers, particularly in resort areas, often have special deals for midweek stays. Check your *AAA TourBook*, if you are a member, or buy a *Mobil Travel Guide* to find special deals.

- BUY IT WHOLESALE.

There are wholesalers and consortiums that sell discount hotel rooms directly to the public. Most full-service travel agencies can book a room through these sources. You may need to make several telephone calls to find an agency that knows what you're talking about; after all, their commission is much larger if they can sell you a full-price room. You may also contact these wholesalers directly. You'll find a list of names and numbers on page 177.

- ASK FOR THE COMMERCIAL RATE.

A commercial hotel or motel rate is usually 30 to 35 percent off the regular price. These rates are supposed to be for anyone traveling on business, but, in reality, if the hotel or motel isn't going to be full anyway, they'll give this commercial rate to anyone, traveling on business or not.

- USE LOWER PRICED, QUALITY HOTELS/MOTELS.

Many hotels and motels are known for their quality at a lesser cost. See page 177 in Resources for a listing of hotels and 800 numbers. Pay special attention to those marked with an asterisk (*). These offer good quality at affordable prices.

SAVE MONEY BY EXCHANGING HOMES—NO COST

You can exchange your apartment, condo or home with someone in your honeymoon destination area by joining a home exchange club. The fee is usually around $50 per year. Your home is listed in a directory, along with those of all the other members. The exchange is very simple: You contact those people who have homes available in the area you would like to visit. The names and numbers of reputable home exchange clubs appear on page 176 in the Resources section.

RENT A CONDO OR PRIVATE HOME – $300/WEEK

One of the best-kept secrets in the travel industry is the availability of condos or private homes for rent by the day or week. The reason your travel agent may not mention these options is probably that there is no sales commission involved. So, how do you find out about these choice accommodations? Call the visitor's bureaus and chambers of commerce for your honeymoon destinations; ask for the names of agencies or companies that handle the rental of private residences or condominiums. Another source is your own church denomination or professional newsletter. Just as an example, the California Teachers' Association has a monthly newsletter with a section called Bulletin Board that is loaded with ads such as these:

Palm Springs Condo – 1/BR, Color TV, Pool, Tennis, Jacuzzi, Security Gate, $65/night or $375/week.

Ski Chalet – Mt. Reba downhill, Bear Valley or Calveras Giant Redwoods. Private Pine Tree Mt. View. Golf Course. Athletic Club Privileges. Ski, Jacuzzi, DW, W/D, Cable TV, Microwave. Beautiful House. $400/week.

Acapulco Small Tropical Villas – 2/BR, garden, pool, $250/week or $40/night.

Here is information from a 40-page booklet called *Myrtle Beach Area Condominium Vacation Guide* that lists condominiums for rent in over 25 complexes along Myrtle Beach:

Arbor House. Quaint Cape Cod designs enhance these spacious 2 bedroom cottages located off Lake Arrowhead Road in the Shore Drive Section of Myrtle Beach. Private pool. Each home has private parking, washer/dryer, fully equipped kitchen, separate dining area. $39 per night or $245 per week.

Shipwatch Pointe. Shore Drive community features several pools and whirlpools, creative landscaping. Convenient to restaurants and numerous golf courses. $35 per night or $220 per week.

There are opportunities like this all over the country; they are worth pursuing when you consider the quality you are getting for the low cost.

RENT AN RV OR HOUSEBOAT – $250 TO $700/WEEK

Here is another bargain for you. How about an RV (recreational vehicle) or houseboat? If you've never tried this type of accommodation, you're in for a treat. Just think – your own self-contained "home" as your honeymoon abode. How special and memorable.

When it comes to RV rentals, check your local yellow pages. Cruise America is a rental company that is highly recommended and has service locations nationwide. Their toll-free number is (800)327-7778. Their smallest unit is 24-feet long, completely self-contained with a full bath, dining room, bedroom and a luxury kitchen that includes a microwave. Cruise America only rents low-mileage units that are clean and in perfect condition.

Houseboats are available wherever there is water, so call the chambers of commerce near your honeymoon destination for names of houseboat rental companies. As an example of what I mean, Beaver Creek Resort on Lake Cumberland in Kentucky is typical. This resort has a full-service marina featuring "luxury" houseboat rentals. Their houseboats have these features:

- Carpeting inside & out.
- Top sundeck.
- Front and top deck furniture.
- Gas grill.
- Cooking and eating utensils.
- Pillows, blankets (bring your own linens).
- Private bath with electric flush toilet.
- Marine band radio and AM/FM radio.
- Life jackets.
- Privacy canvas around the sundeck rail.
- In-line fuel and water gauges.
- Ceiling fan.
- Air conditioning/heat.
- Electric stove/oven.
- Microwave.
- Refrigerator/freezer.

All this for weekly rates starting at about $700 per week.

If you want total privacy and you love the water, a houseboat may be an option. You can always dock it and go onshore for eating out, sightseeing and entertainment.

There are many affordable, yet romantic, honeymoon accommodations available; you just have to know how to ask and where to look. In any case, no matter what the cost, your honeymoon abode will be precious to you, and the memories will last for all the years to come.

CHAPTER 3

YOU GOTTA GET THERE
Affordable Honeymoon Transportation

Now that you've chosen your honeymoon destination, you need a way to get there. The most common choice, of course, is by car. If your own car isn't that trustworthy, you may be able to borrow a more dependable one from a friend or relative. The next best alternative is to rent a car, which we will talk about in chapter 4. Other likely choices are travel by air or rail. One of the main factors in overall honeymoon cost is whether you choose to drive, fly or take a train to your destination. The less expensive honeymoons, although no less fabulous and romantic, don't include expensive transportation costs. However, let's look at ways to save on the more expensive modes of travel.

TRAVEL BY AIR

Between the deregulation of the airline industry in 1978 and the attempt to "restructure" in 1992, the entire market has been thrown into a state of confusion. While researching for this book I spoke with dozens of travel agents, few of whom agreed on flight fares and general cost-cutting strategies. Some of these agents may have deliberately avoided the very lowest fares because of the lower commissions, or perhaps they were trying to suggest the most convenient and least stressful route. If you save $300 apiece on airfare from San Francisco to Miami, but must take three separate flights to do it, the agent may assume you don't want the hassle "just to save $300 per person." However, if you're trying to have the best honeymoon for the least amount of money, you may not mind a little inconvenience; after all — the wedding's over and everything else is bliss, right?

Some travel agents are just too busy or lazy to do the research it takes to come up with the very lowest airfare, and others may be so new on the job they don't have the training required. An added problem is that not all travel agencies are alike. Every agency doesn't necessarily have access to the lowest priced ticket available. So, what can you do to find the best deal? First, read the suggestions that follow.

- BE CAREFUL WHICH CITIES YOU FLY TO AND FROM.
  Most people assume that flights from one general part of the country to another will cost about the same — *wrong*! This is logical, and your first lesson is this: *Airline schedules and fares are not logical!* In order to save money when flying, you must learn to think like the airline executives. For example, the best fares are usually on the *most*

traveled routes. This is where all the competition is between airlines. A round-trip fare from San Francisco to Washington, D.C., for instance, may cost $500; a round-trip fare from San Francisco to Norfolk, Virginia (very close to Washington, D.C.), may cost only $320, a savings of $180 per person. You may plan to rent a car anyway, so you could save $360 by choosing your destination city carefully. I live about a two-hour drive from the Oakland, San Francisco, San Jose and Sacramento airports. Whenever I want to fly, I price out all four and take the best deal. I never consider flights originating from my sparsely populated valley because I will pay twice as much for my ticket.

- SAVE MONEY BY FLYING "CONNECTING" FLIGHTS.

TIPS FOR TRAVELING BY AIR

- Pay for airline tickets with a credit card, not a check or cash.

- Check in at the airport early, even though you may already have boarding passes. And *don't* count on your boarding passes. Always check in anyway. Many airlines don't honor the boarding passes issued by travel agents. They issue seating on a first come, first served basis.

- Bring your luggage on board if you possibly can. This usually means one hanging bag with packing pockets and one small overnight bag for each passenger.

- Reserve your seat assignments as early as allowed by the airline. If you're flying coach and want more legroom, ask for the seats directly behind the bulkhead or next to the emergency exit. Each of these locations will give you at least six inches of extra legroom at no added cost!

The most expensive fares are always for the *nonstop flights*. The next most expensive are *direct flights*, where there will be several stops, but you never get off the airplane. The very cheapest fare, however, is on a *connecting flight*. Most people avoid this type of flight because it means getting off the plane and reboarding another flight, maybe more than once. But, for honeymooners, what difference does it make, right? You're in love! And, after all, another airport is just another romantic adventure, another meal in another restaurant while you wait, and more frequent flyer miles than those earned by the poor souls flying nonstop.

- PLOT YOUR OWN MONEY-SAVING ROUTE.

Another variation of the plan explained above is to devise your own city-hopping route, thus saving even more money. If you make a project out of it and really watch the Sunday travel section of your local newspaper, as well as those of your destination cities (check your local library for current copies), you will find inexpensive special fares from each origination city to certain destinations. You can plot a really economical honeymoon route by flying on two or three specials. This is also known as *split-ticketing*. The fares themselves are known as *promotional fares* and are usually only available for sale for a limited number of days.

Let's say you live in Denver and you want to get to Miami and back. You may discover, through your clever research, that there is a "cheap-cheap special" round-trip fare from Denver to Dallas for only $39. Add to that another $29 round-trip special from Dallas to Atlanta, and a final $49 round-trip from Atlanta to Miami, for a total of only $117 apiece. Compare this to the $358 nonstop round-trip fare you would have had to pay from Denver to Miami, and you'll cut about $482 off your total honeymoon airfare.

No travel agent in his right mind would suggest such a circuitous route, but then, of course, very few of us are into the art of arranging *affordable* honeymoons. If you decide to try this trick, be sure to allow *plenty* of time between flights at each airport, especially if you're changing carriers. And another word of advice: Carry your luggage on board.

There are a couple of other ways to find the cheapest airfares, by the way. One way is to join a discount travel club called Best Fares. It costs about $58 a year and provides monthly updates on cheapest fares to and from all the major cities in the United States. One of the nicest features of this monthly update is the way they keep you informed of several less expensive options. For example, after the Chicago to Cincinnati rate quotes, they may tell you "for lower fare, see Chicago to Dayton." Also, when looking for the cheapest fare from Chicago to Cleveland, they suggest "split fare, see: Chicago to Detroit and Detroit to Cleveland." This lets you know that by doing what I suggest, split-ticketing, you can have a total fare that is less than the direct route. Best Fares telephone number is (800)880-1234.

Another way to find the cheapest fare is to join OAG Electronic Travel Service, the same computerized service used by travel agents. From your computer, you'll need modem access to a telephone line. United States airline information is updated daily on this service, and you can use the information to check for the best fares or to actually book your own reservations. This is one of the great travel bargains around. They charge a one-time hook-up fee of only $25 and a reasonable fee per minute of actual use, which is only about 17 cents a minute if you use the service during non-prime hours. Their telephone number, by the way, is (800)323-3537.

- STAY OVER A SATURDAY NIGHT.

Airlines that cater to business travelers who fly between larger cities usually offer much lower fares to travelers who are willing to stay over a Saturday night, something the business person doesn't want to do. These fares are called *Super Saver Fares*. Here is an example of the savings: A standard coach round-trip from Dallas to Boston *without* a Saturday night stay is about $1,190. The Super Saver Fare round-trip, however, *with* a Saturday night stay is only $421, a savings of $769 per person. As you can see, it may be worth it to you to plan the date of your wedding or the length of your honeymoon to include a Saturday night stay in order to save such a large amount of money.

- COMPARE TRAVEL AGENCIES.

There is a big difference between travel agencies, and even between the agents at the same company. As I've already mentioned, not all agencies have contractual arrangements with the airlines that allow them to offer the lowest fare; not all have agents looking out for *your* best interests; not all have agents who know how to use their travel computer programs; not all have agents who have the patience and diligence required to hunt through the dozens of possibilities to give you the best prices and information; and, unfortunately, not all agents are honest with you. Some may tell you that a fare is the best available when it really isn't. It may be the fare that offers the agent the highest commission—an enticement familiar in any business where the employees buy baby diapers and milk out of their commission checks. So, here are some words of advice regarding travel agencies:

1. Look for an agency that has the System One Corporation's Fare Assurance fare-checking computer program. It searches for and guarantees the lowest airfares available.
2. Call several agencies and ask the same questions; see how their answers compare.
3. Call airlines direct or check your *Best Fares* publication to see how the agencies' answers differ.
4. Try to find a travel agency that is a wholesaler, discount or consolidator agency. This type of agency also has the nickname of "bucket shop" and only sells discounted airline tickets. Using this type of agency can routinely save you from 20 to 70 percent on your airfares. These agencies depend on high volume and remind me of a discount stockbroker because they have no time for warm, fuzzy chitchat over the telephone. They are all business; all they want is an order for the tickets. Then they send you the tickets via certified mail.

   Full-service travel agencies usually don't have access to, or don't *want* to have access to, this type of wholesaler, mainly because of the extremely low sales commissions. But if you contact these discount agents directly, you will be the winner.

   There are several ways to locate these discounters. The first way is through your yellow pages. Look for travel agencies that advertise that they are consolidators, or wholesalers or discounters. Another way is to look in the travel section of your local Sunday newspaper, where agencies advertise in the same way.

- BUY A "HIDDEN-CITY" TICKET.

Remember when I told you that airline fares don't make sense? Well, here's a perfect illustration: You can often save money by purchasing a ticket to a city *farther* away than your actual destination. In other words, if you want to fly from Seattle to Denver, but find that a ticket from Seattle to Chicago, *with a stopover in Denver*, is cheaper, purchase the ticket from Seattle to Chicago and get off in Denver. This trick can often save you hundreds of dollars. This is how to pull this off:

1. Never ask a travel agency to arrange this for you. They know that, although this arrangement is not illegal, airlines frown upon it, and they want to stay in the good graces of the airlines. Therefore, find out about hidden-city routes through other sources, such as Best Fares or OAG Electronic Travel Service, and then go ahead and book the flight, preferably through a discount travel agency. It's up to you to get off at your destination city, which happens to be the stopover city for the airline.

2. Never check your luggage, or it will go on to the final stop without you. *Always carry all luggage on board.*

3. Never try this with round-trip ticketing; book one-way tickets only.

- SAVE MONEY BY BOOKING FARE AHEAD OF TIME.

  You can usually get a lower airline fare by booking in advance. The earlier you book, the more you can save. There are 21-day fares, 7-day fares and 3-day fares. Always ask how much you can save by booking and/or purchasing your fare in advance.

- BEWARE OF AIRLINE TICKET AGENTS.

  Don't ever buy your airline tickets directly from the airline itself. Use their toll-free numbers to get information, but don't actually purchase your tickets from them, because they won't offer you the lower prices available through other sources, such as discount travel clubs, discount and wholesale travel agencies, or even full-service travel agencies. As a matter of fact, airlines will never give you a lower rate than the most expensive travel agency will.

- BUY YOUR TICKETS SECONDHAND.

  Look in the classified ad section of your local newspaper under "Tickets for Sale." You will find very low discounted prices on tickets that were purchased by someone who has decided he or she cannot use them after all. Buying secondhand tickets can be a bit risky, because your name won't be on the ticket, and it can become a problem if you try to check your luggage. Carrying your luggage on board is the only answer here. Secondhand tickets will never work for international travel, because the ticket will be confiscated when it is compared with your name on your passport or ID. If you decide to try this idea for domestic flights, you're on your own. I certainly don't advocate it or guarantee that it will work. If you make it work, however, you can save over a thousand dollars on your total honeymoon expense.

- BUY AS PART OF A PACKAGE OFFER.

  There are a number of ways to receive deep discounts on airline fares by buying tickets in conjunction with something else. Here are just a few examples:

  1. Look for airline discounts available by purchasing goods through a grocery store

or other source. For example, Furr's, a supermarket chain in Texas and New Mexico, made a deal with Continental Airlines. If you purchase at least $24 worth of groceries through their supermarket, you can purchase (at a cost of $5) a certificate entitling you to a 25 percent discount on most Continental flights.

2. American Airlines and the *Home Alone* home video paired up this way: If you buy a *Home Alone* home video you can purchase a discount coupon (at a cost of $1.75) that gives you a $25 to $100 discount on an American Airlines ticket. Isn't that bizarre?

3. If you're under a specified age and apply for a Visa or MasterCard you can receive a certificate that entitles you to fly anywhere USAir flies for only $189 round-trip. See how crazy it gets?

4. Get your airfare for free when it's included in a package trip or as an inexpensive, optional add-on when purchasing a vacation package. For example, a trip package to Tampa, Florida, is offering all of this for one price: round-trip airfare to Tampa via USAir, three nights' accommodations, an Avis rental car with unlimited mileage, three rounds of golf (including cart), full breakfast daily, daily complimentary cocktails and taxes.

This particular vacation package starts at $549 per person and happens to be at the Sheraton Tampa East. There are hundreds of other packages that include airfare; we will discuss them in our chapters on Hawaii, the Caribbean, Mexico and other destinations.

When you purchase a package vacation with airfare as an add-on, the add-on rates are usually extremely low. For example, one package vacation to Hilton Head Island has add-on round-trip airline fares that range from $39 to $176 per person.

TRAVEL BY RAIL

For those of you who want to enjoy each other's company and the scenery, too, you may want to consider honeymooning by train. If your ambition is to get there and get started with the fun, then air travel is great, but for all you sentimental fools, why not ride the rails? Many Americans don't realize there are modern trains, complete with sleeping cars and a variety of restaurants, that traverse all of North America, including Canada and Mexico. When you purchase a train ticket, you can have your "lodging" included in the price, saving you the cost of a hotel or motel, and you can eat quite reasonably by using the train's cafe service or lounge cars. You may also bring your own food on board; you just can't eat it in the formal dining rooms.

TIPS FOR TRAVELING BY RAIL

❧ Make reservations as far ahead of time as possible.

❧ Bring small bills for tipping.

❧ Be sure all your luggage has ID tags that include your name, address and telephone number.

❧ Never assume there is only one train station in a city; there might be two or three.

❧ Don't buy your train tickets from a travel agency, even though the cost is the same to you. In case you decide to cancel your ticket, the agency may balk at refunding your money or may charge you a cancellation fee. Dealing directly with the rail company will help you avoid these problems.

Here are a couple of other things you probably don't know about trains: They even offer movies and bingo. Imagine that!

When it comes to cost, there are about ten variables: whether you are traveling on regular coach, special Club Service or Custom Class (available on some trains on the East Coast and in southern California), the nonstop Metroliner trains (available in the northeastern United States), and whether you reserve a berth, bedroom, etc.

Other cost factors involve discounts, such as Amtrak's All Aboard America Fare (you get a discount if you only travel in a designated third of the United States), Amtrak travel packages, or whether you travel during the summer or not.

Let's say you are planning a summer honeymoon on regular coach fare, but with an economy bedroom (better than a berth, but not as luxurious as the deluxe bedroom), and let's assume you purchase a round-trip ticket that allows you unlimited travel within a third of the United States. You will pay about $189 per person for the coach fare, plus approximately $128 per night for the bedroom. The nice thing about this arrangement is that an economy bedroom includes all meals, which will save on your food budget. Your total cost for a five day, four night honeymoon on the train will run about $1,200, including tips.

The beauty of train travel is that you can arrange your trip to take advantage of stopovers. The only problem is luggage, which you will need to store in a locker at the train station while you enjoy your stopover location. Then, before reboarding another train, get your luggage from the lockers and you're off on another leg of your trip.

If you want to use the train as your transportation to and from your honeymoon destination, the full fare will run between 9 and 30 cents per mile. If you plan ahead, however, you will be able to receive deep discounts, especially through Amtrak's assortment of travel packages. Twice a year Amtrak publishes a *Travel Planner* that lists the bargains available. Call Amtrak at (800)USA-RAIL for all their information.

If you decide to take your honeymoon on a train, I recommend you purchase a book called *Rail Ventures*, published by Rail Ventures Publishing. It is a comprehensive guide to train travel in all of North America, including minute-by-minute route logs, maps, photos, station information, where to stay along the way, and gobs of traveler tips. If you haven't considered train travel before, this book will woo you, and best of all, you will have a honeymoon that you can afford.

Isn't it fun to plan a honeymoon? There are so many cost-cutting options that it is hard to choose, but I know you will make a great decision when it comes to your transportation!

CHAPTER 4

RENT SOME WHEELS
Affordable Car Rentals

Need to rent a car when you arrive at your honeymoon destination? This should be an easy task, but due to the complexity of choices and prices, it may seem overwhelming. Especially when you have more important things on your mind, such as planning a wedding for 300 guests. Here are a few helpful tips from other honeymooners who successfully negotiated the car rental maze before you.

GET THE BEST RATE

There is no such thing as a single, simple price structure for renting a car. You need to do a lot of calling, asking these questions:

- What is the age limit for renting a car from your company?
- What is your best priced deal? Picking the car up on a weekend? Or during the week?
- Is it cheaper to keep a car for a whole week or to rent by the day?
- Is there a drop-off charge for one-way rental?
- Is it cheaper to rent a car at an airport, where most of the rental fleets are parked? Or is the *downtown* rate less expensive?
- How do the rates vary for different sized cars?
- Does your company offer a package deal, in which the rental car is included in a fly-drive combo?
- How can I receive a discount? What if I am an AAA insurance member?
- What are my chances of a free upgrade on certain car classes?
- Is there free, unlimited mileage?
- What is your policy on mandatory refueling charges?
- Do you charge an extra fee if my spouse drives the car?

There are a lot of questions, aren't there? And you *must* ask these questions, because the more questions you ask, the better deal you will get. Car rental companies don't always *offer* the very best deal; you must pull the information out of them.

First of all, a company can be eliminated right away if you don't qualify under their age restrictions. Some companies require the driver be at least 25 years of age; others will rent to a 21-year-old.

When calling for car rental information, always call the actual car rental agencies in your destination city. Don't try to make the arrangements through a travel agent, the nationwide "800" number, or the agency's car rental office in your hometown, unless, of course, you want to rent a car in your hometown. You will find, as you call the different companies, that there will be a multitude of rates and specials. For example, during the fall of 1992 Hertz offered a nationwide rate of only $69 to $99 per week for a subcompact car. Their summer 1992 rates for the same car ranged from $79 to $99 per week, while their rates for a full-size car for that same period ranged from $139 to $159 per week. The reason for the range is that the price varies according to the location. Florida rental rates are usually less than California rates, for example.

You will probably find that the cheapest rates will be by the week, followed by weekend rates, with midweek rates the highest. The drop-off rates will vary according to where you pick up and drop off the car. These charges used to be in the $75 to $100 range, but have recently climbed at some locations to $300, $400 or more. These extra charges may be waived, however, if you are headed to a city where the agency needs more cars, such as certain cities in California and Florida.

The best car rental rates are usually found at airports where a fleet of cars are parked, as opposed to a downtown location where parking is at a premium. This can vary, however, so be sure to ask.

There are basically seven classes of cars offered by car rental companies. Here they are listed in order by price, starting with the least expensive:

- Subcompact
- Compact
- Intermediate
- Full-size four-door
- Minivan
- Luxury
- Convertible

Once you have selected a class of car, ask if there are any combination deals available. There are often fly-drive packages, or discounts on other combinations, such as Disneyland specials that combine airfare, car rental and hotel in one affordable package.

Along this same line, you should ask about any other discounts. For example, if you are a member of the California State Automobile Association, you will receive a discount when you rent a Hertz or Avis car at most of their rental locations. An added bonus is that, as a CSAA member, you will also receive free extended personal liability protection when you rent one of these cars.

You can receive other types of discounts by booking ahead or in conjunction with airline reservations. Hertz, for example, offers discounted rates under their Book Ahead plan which requires you make the reservation at least three days in advance and have a current airline ticket. Their Same Day plan has a rate of $28.99 for an economy car, but this requires a two-day advance reservation and a current airline ticket.

An example of discount combinations is the deal offered by Outrigger Hotels in Hawaii. If you stay at the Outrigger Reef in Waikiki or the Royal Waikoloan on the Big Island, you will receive a free rental car from Dollar Rent A Car included in the cost of your room. You must ask for the Free Ride package when you make your hotel reservations.

One last suggestion for saving money on car rentals: Rent from a smaller rental company that may have older cars. This can save you up to 50 percent.

As you can see, there are many ways to rent an affordable car for your honeymoon. The problem is that the clerk at a car rental agency won't necessarily suggest the best cost-cutting options when you call, so it is up to you to ask questions!

Remember—the more questions you ask in all of your travel planning, the better deal you will get! This holds true for airline travel, hotel accommodations, cruising, car rentals, train travel, and every other type of reservation you make. Ask, ask, ask! By asking every question you will find the best deal. All you need is plenty of patience and the time to call every car rental agency. There is a complete listing of car rental companies in the Resources section in the back of this book. Use this list to do your homework, and, meanwhile, watch for ads in newspapers and on television.

When you're doing your calling, be sure to ask about mileage charges, too. Many companies offer unlimited mileage, while others charge so much per mile. Still others offer free mileage up to a certain amount, such as 100 miles, then charge a per-mile fee.

Ask if there is an extra fee for your spouse to be able to drive the car. If your spouse doesn't meet the age requirement, or if the fee is out of line, you will be the only driver allowed.

ABOUT RENTAL CAR INSURANCE

Beware of car rental agencies that try to pressure you into buying their CDW (Collision Damage Waiver) insurance. Legislation has recently been passed in a number of states eliminating the sale of CDWs. In California a law was passed that limits the price of a CDW to $9 a day, but requires the car rental company tell you that you're probably already covered on your own insurance. Usually a CDW offers only limited protection and is a better deal for the rental company than for the motorist. Call your insurance agent to see if a rental car is covered for collision on your regular auto insurance policy. A rental car *is* probably covered, and if so don't be coerced into buying one of these CDWs from a car rental company. This will save you $9 to $17 a day. The car rental agency will try their best to scare you into purchasing this coverage, however, because it is one of their major profit centers.

If you find that a rental car is *not* covered on your auto insurance, check with your credit card issuer. Collision Damage Insurance is included as a membership benefit with some American Express, Diners Club, Gold MasterCards and Gold VISA cards. Also, some regular VISA and MasterCards offer this benefit as well. If none of your card memberships offer this free insurance, it may be worth your while to apply for a VISA card through Chase Manhattan Bank. Their card offers this insurance free to its members. As the card costs only $20 a year and CDW averages about $12 a day, getting one of these cards may be worth the money.

PRECAUTIONS WHEN RENTING A CAR

First of all, check for any body damage on your rental car before driving it out of the agency's lot. If you find a dent, other interior or exterior damage or any missing accessory, such as the tape deck, ask the agent to record this on your rental agreement. Be sure you both initial this information.

Test the car before driving off. Drive it around the parking lot to be sure everything is in working order. Try the windshield wipers, radio, lights, horn, etc. If the car isn't operating properly, turn it in for one that is.

Get the emergency service telephone number of the car rental firm. Find out if they have 24-hour service. One honeymooning couple took off in a car that broke down at their destination, which happened to be Palm Springs, California. They were driving down the main street of Palm Springs when the car died and wouldn't restart. They called the number for National Car Rental (the company they rented from) who sent someone to pick them up, take them to their fleet rental counter at the Palm Springs airport, and issue them another car. It was hardly an inconvenience, but only because they had the National Car Rental toll-free number handy.

The last bit of advice is this: Be sure to write down the license number of the rental car you're driving. You'd be surprised how many people lose their rental cars in parking lots because they don't recognize them on sight.

Because you have read this chapter you will avoid a lot of grief. You'll know what to watch for, what questions to ask, and how to avoid being pressured into purchasing CDW insurance.

I know you'll find a terrific deal on your special honeymoon car.

CHAPTER 5

You Need to Keep Up Your Strength
Affordable Honeymoon Dining

You're making progress! Your reservations are made for your airline tickets, accommodations and rental car—all at the least cost for the best quality. Now, let's talk food!

One of the neat things about honeymooners is that you are so easy to please. You've had a breathtaking wedding, fun-filled reception, and now you have each other's company for the rest of your lives. Is this heaven, or what? At this point there isn't a meal anywhere in town that won't stir your emotions. Even a Big Mac will do the trick; all you need is something to fill your tummies as you go through your days. But for the sake of this chapter, let's *assume* you really care about your epicurean experiences; let's *assume* you really care whether a restaurant has a seductive ambiance.

Avoid "Tourist Traps"

Most of the honeymooners I interviewed advised against "tourist" restaurants. They also avoided restaurants in their hotel. These types of dining facilities are usually overpriced, overcrowded and impersonal. What you want to look for are those intimate cafes, smaller specialty restaurants, ethnic spots, and favorites of the "natives." You need a quiet table where you can talk and enjoy tasty dishes and personalized service. You can have all this and more by doing just a little homework.

Step one is to do your research before you leave on your honeymoon. Start with the *AAA TourBooks* or the *Mobil Travel Guides*. These helpful guides will list the best local restaurants in each town. Watch for descriptions such as: "intimate Victorian decor," "small Italian cafe featuring candlelight and ocean views." Avoid these descriptions: "all you can eat," "cafeteria-style," "specializing in children's menu," "excellent family restaurant." These guidebooks also indicate quality and prices. The idea is to find a restaurant that is suitably romantic and has the highest rating for the most affordable prices. All this research can be done ahead of time, including calling the restaurant itself and asking plenty of questions.

Your next best source is to ask the locals at your destination. Don't ask the "old folks"; they may think Luby's Cafeteria is ideal. Search out natives in your age bracket, such as the hotel desk clerk, rental car agent, bank teller, etc. Tell them you are on your honeymoon and want a sensual little spot, good food and affordable prices. Their recommendations may match the research you have already done, but it is still a good idea to ask their advice.

Some of the best choices will be restaurants featuring fresh local and regional foods. For example, if you're in Louisiana, look for a little seafood restaurant specializing in crawfish. If you're in San Francisco, try the crab.

Make Lunch Your Main Meal

If you're really determined to try a famous, upscale restaurant, see if they're open for lunch. Usually you will be able to order the same items that are offered on the dinner menu, but for half the price. Another alternative is to call ahead and ask if the lunch menu is available during the dinner hour; often it is, but only upon request.

Make a Meal off the Appetizer Menu

This is an idea that has become quite popular lately, whether on a honeymoon or not. We live near the San Francisco Bay Area, and when we eat in the city we often order from the appetizer menu. It's amazing how much money you can save when you don't order a full meal, but you will fill up just the same. Some of the specialty items on upscale appetizer menus may be soups (baked French onion is my favorite—a meal in itself), salads, deep-fried zucchini or cheeses, breads or small pasta dishes. It is considered perfect etiquette to order in this manner, so don't feel intimidated by the waiter. This way you can experience the cuisine for about a third of the price.

A Picnic for Two

Why not take a picnic to some secluded spot? What could be more sensual than a view, a blanket, and a basket filled with wine, cheeses, meats, fruits, breads, olives and specialty dishes bought at a local deli or market? You'll not only have fun shopping, but you'll have special memories of your picnics, at a fourth of the cost of eating out.

Tip: If someone asks you what you need as a wedding gift, suggest a picnic basket complete with plastic plates, cups, wine carrier, etc. Or how about an ice chest or thermos? You will appreciate the practicality; after all, how many fake silver trays can you use your first 10 years of marriage?

Caution: When packing a picnic lunch, there are a few precautions to take. The USDA's Meat and Poultry hotline has these suggestions: Pack *cold* food in an insulated cooler. Keep the cooler *inside* your car, not in the trunk. When you arrive at your site, keep the lid on the cooler and avoid repeated openings. Forget creamy foods such as rice pudding or custard pies.

By the way, you can save money by keeping an ice chest full of goodies all day long, whether in your car or hotel room. How about canned pop, single-serving cans of juice, fresh fruits and vegetables, breads, cheeses, crackers or candy?

You may also want to consider taking along an electric coil or small electric pot so you can make your own coffee or tea in your motel room. Or, how about instant soups or hot chocolate?

FILL UP FOR FREE

Why not take advantage of free food? There are several ways to pull this off.

The most obvious way is to go on a package trip that includes a certain number of meals. For example, certain package plans specify "two meals per day" or "breakfast included." If you take a cruise, which we will discuss later in this book, all your meals will be included in one price.

Also, many hotels and motels are now including continental breakfasts. Some of these breakfasts are more complete than others, but take advantage of whatever they offer. My husband and I always look for this cost-cutter where we can save a total of $10 to $12 on breakfast for the two of us, not counting an extra 15 percent for a tip! Some hotels, motels or inns offer a complete breakfast, while others only provide rolls, juice and coffee. We are grateful for whatever we can get. If you don't like the crowded atmosphere of the dining room itself, take your plate out by the pool, patio, or back to your room.

The bed-and-breakfast idea, which we talked about in chapter 2, is an obvious winner because breakfast is always included in the room price.

Fill up on free breakfasts and you won't be overly hungry by lunch. You may even be able to get by on a snack at midday and hold off your spending until your dinner meal.

Another trick honeymooners are using to "fill-up-for-free" is the happy-hour buffet. I had never thought of this, but obviously a lot of people have. They go to a cocktail lounge where drinks are priced two-for-one. They order a couple of Cokes and fill up on the appetizers. Some of the appetizers are actually meals, such as do-it-yourself burritos, or egg rolls, cocktail wienies, salads, breads, sliced melons, chips and dips or barbecued chicken wings. If you can resist ordering a lot of expensive drinks, your total tab for dinner for two can be about $3. Is that a deal, or what?

FIND A NICER CHAIN RESTAURANT

Consumer Reports magazine recently did a poll among their readers to rate "restaurant chains that are a cut above fast food." Here are 10 of their choices:

- Baker's Square (noted for their pies),
- Chili's (an authentic, fun Mexican restaurant),
- Cracker Barrel Restaurants (replete with fireplaces, exposed beams, antiques and Americana),

- Marie Callender's (high class with reasonable prices),
- Olive Garden Restaurants (Italian food and atmosphere, including "Arrivederci Roma" playing over the public-address system),
- Po Folks (relaxing atmosphere with home-cooked meals),
- Ponderosa Restaurants (excellent steak houses with privacy created by high walls between diners),
- Sizzler's Restaurants (frequently feature two sirloin steak dinners for a total of $8.99),
- Stuart Anderson's (every table or booth is enclosed for privacy—the honeymooners' delight), and
- T.G.I. Fridays (trendy pub with booths, polished brass and Tiffany lamps).

Look for That Sidewalk Cafe

Many of the honeymooners I interviewed recommended the sidewalk cafe. Depending on your honeymoon destination, this could be a great idea! If you're in Vail, Colorado, La Jolla, California or Daytona Beach, Florida, you can enjoy an affordable meal as you watch the world go by. Some of these cafes can get a little pricey, so check out the menu first. Many, however, offer bratwurst and German potato salad at $3.99, or fish and chips for the same. Keep an eye out for these affordable spots.

Split a Meal

Unless the restaurant ranks highly in the guidebooks, you can split a meal without fear of embarrassment. This has become quite common, especially in ethnic restaurants. It is only logical to divide a Chinese meal or a Mexican fajita or a large pizza. Look for the obvious and the two of you can eat for one fare. When my husband and I order a fajita we ask for two extra tortillas (usually provided at no extra charge), and we actually waddle out of the restaurant, we are so full. Most restaurants have one or two menu items that are grossly oversized and can easily feed two people. Ask the waiter or waitress for advice.

I have given you plenty of affordable honeymoon dining ideas to choose from. As I said in the beginning, you newlyweds are easy to please, but you might as well have the best cuisine for the least expense. That way you will have money for all the other fun stuff you'd like to see and do. Happy eating!

CHAPTER 6

Freeloading Fun!
Free Honeymoon Entertainment

It's almost as easy to entertain honeymooning couples as it is to feed them. A hot dog and a steak taste pretty much the same when you're on your honeymoon; likewise, it doesn't take a lot of money to entertain you either. In this chapter we will discover the exciting world of free attractions. There are literally thousands of places to see and things to do that are not only fun and amusing, but memorable as well. Browse through the many ideas that follow.

Free Festivals

There are local and regional festivals going on all over the country on any given day of the week. These festivals are a lot of fun, it's easy to get caught up in the spirit, and, best of all, they are free.

Just as an example of what I mean, take the Bodega Bay Fisherman's Festival in Bodega Bay, California, a sincere little ocean community a couple of hours north of San Francisco. Every April they hold a festival, usually over a weekend, and it's guaranteed to entertain. It all starts with the blessing of the fleet and ends with the bathtub race in the harbor. The whale watching, arresting sunsets and crisp salt air are thrown in as a bonus.

Free Museums and Exhibits

You know how it is in the workaday world, you never have time to soak up some culture. Even if an exhibit comes to your hometown, you probably can't enjoy it because it requires *time*, something you finally have plenty of on vacation, and, after all, a honeymoon *is* a vacation, too. So, why not take advantage of your free time to truly enjoy some of the great museums and exhibits along your honeymoon route? There are hundreds of types, including the more common museums of natural history. Here are just a few of the special categories of museums: Civil War history, cable car, farm implement, aviation, old lighthouse, railroad, old schoolhouse, fire fighters', logging, Indian, blacksmith, shipyard, marine, dinosaur and clock.

Exhibits include art and photography, as well as crafts and hobbies. If you happen onto a large university, you can ask whose work is being shown. A campus of the California State University located in my hometown has continual exhibits; they recently displayed Ansel Adams's black-and-white photography, on loan from an out of state source. What an excellent use of time, and again, it's free entertainment.

Historical Sites

There are some very interesting spots dotted all over our country, including missions, Indian ruins, buildings (for example, Robert Frost's cabin), covered bridges (on the National Register), battle sites, national monuments, ghost towns and historical homes. These sites can fill your days with fascinating revelations, most of which you will want to photograph. (Ask for a decent camera as a wedding gift.)

Walking Tours

Along this vein are planned walking tours. Many chambers of commerce conduct walking tours of their cities, and if they don't, make up one of your own. Include all the sights you want to see, from the local Chinatown to the public gardens, planetarium, aquariums, zoo, observatory, and the "old town" streets and alleys. One of the most pleasurable afternoons of my life was spent on a walking tour of old Santa Fe, New Mexico.

Be a Sports Fan

In chapter 25 I'll talk about participation sports, but it can also be fun to watch others, especially when it comes to things like parasailing, hang gliding, bungee jumping, parachuting or surfing. It's even fun to watch a bowling or softball tournament, or golfers as they hit approach shots to the finishing green at an upscale golf course. And how about all those halls of fame peppered around the country? There will probably be one close by that you can visit for free, from the National Track and Field Hall of Fame to the ones dedicated to rodeo performers, or to football or baseball players. Depending on how much you enjoy certain sports, it can be a real treat to spend an afternoon in one of these buildings.

Commercial Tours

Why not take advantage of the free tours offered by commercial establishments? If you're honeymooning in California, for example, you won't want to miss visiting several wineries. There are hundreds of other stores and factories that offer tours, from outlets producing cheeses or honey, to creameries, to Christmas shops full of candies and decorations. Just be sure to pick a tour that won't put you to sleep, and if you've just finished up a college or professional course of study, you may want to bypass this whole idea. It can seem awfully educational unless you're in a festive mood.

Free Concerts

What can be more relaxing than lying on a blanket in a park listening to a free pops concert? Or free recitals or jazz performances at the local university? Or, how about all the music that's included with the festivals you may discover here and there? Small-town America offers free weekend concerts throughout the summer, such as the weekly band concert at a lakeside park in Rice Lake, Wisconsin.

ENJOY THE SIGHTS!

This is too obvious to mention, but don't forget the thrill of living in the moment. No brochure can describe the feeling of actually being there. Plan your honeymoon so it includes as much scenic pleasure as possible, whether the exhilaration of Niagara Falls, the smooth sensation of a free ferry ride across the Mississippi River, or the elation you feel as you lean over the south rim of the Grand Canyon.

You have hundreds of free activities to choose from, but how do you find out about all the festivals, walking tours, musical concerts and the rest? There are several excellent sources. One is a book entitled *Guide to Free Attractions*, published by Cottage Publications. Also, contact the chambers of commerce and visitor's bureaus for all the towns and cities you will be visiting. *Motorland* magazine (for American Automobile Association members) offers up-to-date calendars of free events, and the *Mobil Travel Guide* is filled with ideas. The newspaper entertainment section of your destination city is always a good source, particularly their Friday and Sunday editions.

There is plenty for you to do and see that is completely free, but in order to take advantage of these ideas, you must plan ahead. The more work you do ahead of time, the more free honeymoon fun you will have. It's there for the taking—you just have to know where to look!

CHAPTER 7

HELPFUL HINTS
Free Honeymoon Advice

Everyone thinks they have great advice for the honeymooning couple, but here is some of the best, gleaned from experts as well as experienced honeymooners.

PACKING TIPS

- Carry medication, travel documents and tickets in your carry-on luggage.
- Pack heavy items (shoes, books, hair dryer) around the edge of your suitcase.
- Use zip-top plastic bags for all liquid toiletries.
- Fill the spaces in your suitcases with rolled-up socks, underwear, sweaters, T-shirts, lingerie, etc.
- Use every nook and cranny of space, even tuck small items into the shoes you are packing.
- Pack a fold-up tote bag for any purchases you may make.
- Pack at least one pair of *comfortable* walking shoes, even if they are "ugly."
- Pack a small sewing kit.
- Don't pack aerosol cans.

HEALTH TIPS

- If you have a sensitive stomach and anything a little different tends to upset it, take along some Pepto-Bismol. It can provide welcome relief because it stabilizes your system by actually killing bacteria. Some of its cousins are Kaopectate, Donnagel, Quiagel or Rheaban.
- Another emergency over-the-counter drug is called Monistat 7, a godsend for any woman experiencing an itch, especially common in humid climates.
- To prevent motion sickness, ask your doctor about "the patch" worn behind one ear. It contains medication released slowly over a three-day period. The brand name is Transderm Scop.
- To prevent jet lag, heed these precautions:
  —Get into the sunshine soon after your arrival. It will help stabilize your sleep cycle.
  —Wear comfortable, loose clothing during flight.
  —Try to exercise during a flight, even if it means a few hikes up and down the aisle.

—Don't overeat or drink heavily during the flight.

- If you (heaven forbid!) have a cold on your honeymoon, take a decongestant before a flight to help clear your ears and sinus passages.
- Check with your doctor before taking your honeymoon. Ask about all the medications suggested in this chapter, as well as copies of any prescriptions that you may want to have with you on your trip.
- Bring a copy of your contact lens prescription; in case you lose your contact lenses, you can always have a new set made up while you're on your honeymoon.
- Pack a small first-aid kit with the basics: a pain reliever, athlete's foot medication, bandages, suntan lotion, antacid tablets, calamine lotion (for skin irritations or poison ivy), water purification tablets, an antiseptic lotion and insect repellant.

Tipping

- Waiters or waitresses: 15 percent of the bill, not including the tax.
- Concierge: $5 to $10 for special services he may provide.
- Doorman: $1 for hailing your taxi.
- Room service: 15 percent of the bill.
- Valet parking: $1 to $2 when you leave or pick up your car.
- Limousine chauffeur: tip is always included in the bill; no additional tip is necessary.
- Taxi driver: 15 percent of the total fare.
- Hotel or motel housekeeper: $1 to $2 per day. (It is a good idea to leave your largest tips at the beginning of your stay, for obvious reasons.)
- Hotel pool attendant: 50 cents for furnishing you with a towel.
- Train redcap: 50 cents per bag.
- Train sleeping car attendant: $1 per night per person.
- Train dining car: 15 percent of bill.

Lost Baggage

- The best prevention for lost baggage is to carry your bags on board the plane with you.
- When you must check your bags:
  —Make a detailed list of the contents of each bag; keep this list with you as you board the flight.
  —Place name and address tags on the *inside* and outside of each bag. Always use your business, not personal, address. Also, put some identifying mark on your bags to prevent someone from accidentally claiming your bag. I use bathtub stickers on my

bags, but you might want to run a red-striped tape around each bag, or tie a colorful ribbon or pom-pom to your suitcase handles.

— Lock your bags.

— *Watch* and see with your own eyes that the correct bag tag has been placed on your bags so they arrive at your destination.

— Upon arrival of your flight, go to the baggage claim area *immediately*!

— If your bag isn't on the carousel, don't panic. Do notify the baggage service personnel right away, but probably your bag will arrive on the next flight, which could be within an hour of your flight's arrival. Most bags arrive within 24 hours, but it is smart for the bride to pack one complete outfit and a few essentials in the groom's bag and vice versa. That way you'll get by until your bag is located.

— If your bag never does show up, the airline is liable and must reimburse you a certain amount per bag. This amount varies from about $500 to $750 per bag, so if the contents are worth more than that, you may want to purchase additional insurance at the check-in counter.

OTHER CRISES

- If you miss your cruise, you can charter a launch or fly to the next port.
- If you miss your plane or train, call ahead and release your seats. Book the next available flight or train.
- If the hotel or motel has no record of your reservation, ask to speak to the *manager*, not the desk clerk. Show your confirmation slip, mention that you are on your honeymoon and request compensation. The manager will probably give you an upgraded room at no additional cost or arrange for a comparable room at another hotel.

DON'T GET RIPPED OFF

All travelers are prey to the thief; however, honeymooners can become understandably preoccupied and are especially vulnerable. Here are some precautions:

- Don't carry cash; carry traveler's checks or credit cards.
- Leave all unnecessary credit cards at home; only take those you will use.
- Never put all your cash or traveler's checks in one pocket or purse; spread them out: some in an inside pocket, some in a purse, some locked in the hotel safe. *Men*: Never carry your wallet in your back pocket.
- Use your ATM card to draw cash as you go along; this way you can avoid having to carry credit cards, cash or traveler's checks. Before leaving on your honeymoon, find

out where the automatic teller machines are located at your destinations; your bank or credit union will furnish you with this list of ATM locations.

- Never leave your hotel key in view while you're swimming, dining or sunbathing. Always zip it away in an inconspicuous place.
- Once the hotel or motel maid has made up your room, leave the television on and a "Do Not Disturb" sign on your door. Don't leave valuables in the room; take them with you or lock them in the hotel safe.
- When inside your room, place a wedge of wood firmly under the door. Thieves may try to enter while you are showering or sleeping. Always use the sliding lock or deadbolt when you're inside your room.
- Don't leave luggage, camera, purse or clothing in the passenger compartment of your car. Always lock things away in your trunk.
- Watch out for the "honeymoon squeeze," in which one thief engages you in conversation or bumps into you to distract you while the accomplice picks your pocket or steals your luggage.

CONTINGENCY FUND

Tuck away an emergency fund. Let's say you have added all your anticipated honeymoon expenses, including your spending and miscellaneous money, and you have this amount in traveler's checks or in a checking account accessible through your ATM card. In addition to that money, hide away an extra $50 or $100, partly in small bills; fold the bills over and slide them into a secret compartment of your wallet or purse. After all, emergencies do happen, and you will be thrilled to have that extra money to pull out—just in case.

In all the years I've been traveling, I've never been ripped off, nor has any other frightful thing happened; I'm sure that is because I'm aware of the things that *can* happen, and I take precautions. My worst incident was when my luggage didn't arrive when I did; however, it was on the next flight, so all my panic was a waste of energy. Just be cool and confident, and you'll be fine.

A ROMANTIC HONEYMOON IN YOUR OWN HOME STATE

CHAPTER 8

THE LAND OF LOVABLE FRUITS AND NUTS
Affordable California Honeymoons

HONEYMOON NO. 1 — FT. BRAGG — MENDOCINO

Route
- Highway 101 north of San Francisco to Willits.
- Highway 20 west to Ft. Bragg at Highway 1.
- Highway 1 south 10 miles to Mendocino.

Romantic Appeal
- Remote communities with European flavor and unparalleled ocean scenery. An artists' mecca with restored nineteenth-century buildings and homes.

Free Attractions
- Hiking in the Yolla Bolly-Middle Eel Wilderness area.
- Seals, sea lions and whale watching.
- Walks along the beach.
- Art exhibits.
- Private picnics in hidden coves.
- Kelly House Historical Museum.

Low-Cost Attractions
- Mendocino Coast Botanical Gardens (17 acres of woods, meadows and gardens, Fern Canyon, and a one-mile loop trail to the Pacific Ocean). Cost: $5.
- Rent a bicycle built for two.
- Find an affordable restaurant with an ocean view — there are several on the bay in Ft. Bragg and in the town of Mendocino.

Special Splurges
- The Skunk Railroad (California Western) — A 40-mile round-trip through redwood groves and over the Noyo River. Cost: $18.50 per person.
- Have at least one meal at one of the pricier restaurants that overlooks the ocean.

HONEYMOON NO. 2 — THE WINE COUNTRY —
BODEGA BAY — JENNER

Route
- Highway 101 north out of San Francisco to Petaluma.
- Highway 116 east out of Petaluma to Napa.
- Highway 29 north out of Napa. Takes you through Napa Valley to the town of Calistoga.
- Highway 128 north out of Calistoga back to Highway 101.
- Highway 101 south to Santa Rosa.
- Highway 116 east through Guerneville to Jenner (on the Pacific Ocean).
- Highway 1 south along the ocean to Bodega Bay.
- Highway 1 east to Sebastopol.
- Highway 12 from Sebastopol back to Highway 101.

Romantic Appeal
- The sensuality of Napa Valley, with its vineyards, rolling hills and adventures.
- Nostalgic Americana of Calistoga, Guerneville, Bodega Bay and Sebastopol.
- The passion of the Pacific's waves and surf.

Free Attractions
- Winery tours and wine tastings on Highway 29, through the Napa Valley for 28 miles, from Napa to Calistoga.
- Five different walking tours of Napa (maps available at Napa City Hall, Second and School streets).
- Sharpsteen Museum in Calistoga.
- Walking tour of Sebastopol.
- Soak up the sunset while watching the fishermen unload their catches on the docks at Bodega Bay.
- Whale-watch from the point at Bodega Bay.

Low-Cost Attractions
- Tram ride from Highway 29 to the Sterling Winery. Cost: $5.
- Side trip 12 miles north of Jenner to Fort Ross State Historical Park (established by the Russians in 1812). Cost: $5.
- Petrified Forest (5 miles west of Calistoga). Cost: $3.

Special Splurges
- Hot-air balloon rides over Napa Valley. One-hour ride, including champagne, starts at $120 per person.
- Napa Valley Wine Train ride (36-miles long). Cost: $29.

- Side trip south of Napa to Vallejo to see Marine World Africa, U.S.A. Cost: Approx. $21.
- Any meal at any of the restaurants at Silverado Country Club Resort in Napa. Cost: $15 and up.
- Calistoga mud bath, followed by a soak in geothermal mineral water. Cost: $38.
- Calistoga massages. Cost: $32.

HONEYMOON NO. 3 — CARLSBAD — SAN DIEGO — TIJUANA

Route
- Highway 5 south of Los Angeles to Carlsbad.
- Highway 5 south of Carlsbad to La Jolla and San Diego.
- Highway 5 or 805 south of San Diego to Tijuana, Mexico.

Romantic Appeal
- White sand beaches.
- Exciting restaurants, shopping and scenery.
- Delight and diversity of old Mexico.

Free Attractions
- Walking tour along the beach in Carlsbad.
- Ocean scenery along the entire route.
- Scripps Aquarium and Museum at the Scripps Institute of Oceanography, La Jolla Shores Drive, La Jolla.
- Free entertainment at the Bazaar Del Mundo in Old Town State Park, San Diego, including Mexican folk dancing on Saturdays from 1 to 4 P.M. and Flamenco dancing on Sundays from 1 to 4 P.M.
- Firehouse Museum, San Diego.
- Gaslamp Quarter (16 block re-creation of the Victorian era in downtown San Diego). Has international restaurants, boutiques, antique stores and restored 1880s buildings.
- Picnicking and swimming at Mission Bay Park, near downtown San Diego.
- All the free attractions at Balboa Park, San Diego, including:
  - Botanical Building.
  - Spanish Village Art Center.
  - Tinken Art Gallery.
  - House of Pacific Relations (15 cottages representing 29 nationalities). Music and dance programs given free on Sundays from 2 to 3 P.M. during the summer.
  - Amateur performers, including mimes, jugglers, musicians and magicians.
  - Terrific people-watching locations — all kinds of characters about including trick skateboarders and rollerbladers.

- Seaport Village entertainment complex at Kettner Boulevard and West Harbor Drive. Dining, shopping and entertainment at a harborside setting. The San Diego Symphony gives free evening concerts June through August, complete with fireworks.
- Take a walking tour of La Jolla, just north of San Diego, including the beach parks, downtown and ocean cliffs.
- If you can't afford to take in Sea World, watch their fireworks on summer evenings for free from Mission Bay or Ocean Beach.

Low-Cost Attractions
- Several days' worth of fun at Balboa Park, including:

—Aerospace Historical Center	Cost: $4
—Hall of Champions Sports Museum	Cost: $3
—Rueben Fleet Space Theater	Cost: $6
—San Diego Auto Museum	Cost: $3.50
—San Diego Model Railroad Museum	Cost: $1.50
—San Diego Museum of Art	Cost: $5
—San Diego Museum of Man	Cost: $3
—San Diego Natural History Museum	Cost: $5
—San Diego Zoo	Cost: $10.75

- Junipero Serra Museum, Old Town San Diego. Cost: $3.
- Guided walking tour of Old Town San Diego. Cost: $2.
- Cabrillo National Monument at south end of Cabrillo Memorial Drive on Highway 209, including 1855 lighthouse. Cost: $1.
- Maritime Museum of San Diego, on the Embarcadero in San Diego. Cost: $5.
- Mission Basilica San Diego on San Diego Mission Road in Mission Valley. Cost: $1.
- Old Town Trolley Tours offer a one-and-a-half-hour—trolley bus excursion to many sites, including Balboa Park, Seaport Village, Old Town, etc. Cost: $14.
- *Bahia Belle*, a sternwheeler, cruises Mission Bay. Cost: $5.
- Invader Cruises, narrated tours of San Diego Harbor. Cost: $9-15.
- Rent a bicycle or paddle boat. Cost: $4 per hour and up.
- Spend a day in Tijuana, Mexico, where your American dollars will go a long way. Bring your Christmas list.

Special Splurges
- Sea World on Mission Bay in San Diego. Cost: $22.95 per person.
- Any meal in the oceanfront dining room at the Sea Lodge at La Jolla Shores in La Jolla. Cost: Entrees start at about $16.
- Lunch or dinner at the Top O' the Cove Restaurant in La Jolla on Prospect Street. Dramatic ocean views. Cost: Entrees start at about $18.

HONEYMOON NO. 4 — CATALINA ISLAND

Route

- Can be reached by sea. Various cruise boats offer departures to Catalina Island from Long Beach, Redondo, San Pedro, Newport Beach and San Diego.
- Can also be reached by air via small aircraft or helicopters that leave from Long Beach, San Pedro and Costa Mesa.

Romantic Appeal

- The pristine allure of a preserved island with a fragile and protected environment.
- The exquisite beauty and sensual feeling of being hidden from the rest of the world.

Free Attractions

- Catalina Island Museum in the Casino.
- Walking tour of Avalon and the beaches.

Low-Cost Attractions

- Avalon Scenic Tour. Cost: $5.
- Casino Tour. Cost: $6.
- Catalina Adventure Tours (glass-bottom boat trips). Cost: $5.50.
- Coastal Cruise to Seal Rocks. Cost: $5.
- Flying Fish Boat Trip (see nocturnal flying fish by use of searchlights). One-hour night tour. Cost: $6.
- Island Safari (two-and-a-half-hour guided motor tour). Cost: $15.50.
- Skyline Drive Tour (views of Avalon and the island's interior). Cost: $10.50.
- Snorkeling Safari (a two-hour snorkeling and diving trip). Cost: $15 including gear.
- Rent a bicycle. Cost: About $5 per hour. (A permit is needed to go biking in the interior.)

Special Splurges

- Twilight Dining at Two Harbors (a 14-mile coastline cruise that includes a buffet and a guided hike). Cost: $35 per person.
- Have at least one meal at Pirrone's overlooking the harbor at Avalon. The restaurant features Italian food and seafood specialties, as well as prime rib. Cost: Entrees start at about $25.

Note: See chapter 27 for special features on San Francisco and Los Angeles.

CHAPTER 9

THE LAND OF REVERENT RAINBOWS
Affordable Honeymoons in the Pacific Northwest
Oregon, Washington and Idaho

OREGON

HONEYMOON NO. 1 — THE OREGON COAST

Route
- Highway 5 north of Grants Pass to Highway 42.
- Highway 42 west to Bandon, on the Pacific Ocean.
- Follow Highway 101 north up the coast of Oregon, through Coos Bay, North Bend, Reedsport, Florence, Waldport and as far as Newport.
- Highway 20 west out of Newport back to Highway 5.

Romantic Appeal
- Photogenic shorelines, including lighthouses, cliffs, rocks, bays, marine life and immense, crashing waves.
- Mild temperatures, perfect for honeymooners.
- When the fog rolls in or the winds pick up, cozy up to a crock of clam chowder at a cafe on a bay.
- Dig your toes into the sand and cuddle as you watch the sun set over the Pacific.

Free Attractions
- River's End Gallery—free exhibits in the Old Coast Guard Building in Bandon.
- Walking tour of Bandon's Old Town, Coos Bay's historical residential area, North Bend, Reedsport, Florence, Waldport and the Old Bay Front, a waterfront section of Newport.
- Coos Art Museum, 235 Anderson Avenue, Coos Bay.
- Golden and Silver Falls State Park, 24 miles northeast of Coos Bay.
- Beachcombing, hiking and crabbing on a 46-mile stretch of public beach from Coos Bay to Tillamook, including the Oregon Dunes National Recreation Area north of North Bend and Coos Bay.
- Devil's Punch Bowl, 8 miles north of Newport (a rock formation that fills from below with a roar at high tide).
- Hatfield-Marine Science Center on Marine Science Drive on Yaquina Bay in Newport. This is a facility of Oregon State University which offers whale-watching programs in the spring and winter.

- Lincoln County Historical Society Museums, 545 Southwest Ninth Street, Newport.
- Newport Art Center at the Nye Beach turnaround, Newport.

Low-Cost Attractions
- Bandon Historical Society Museum in the Old Coast Guard Building. Cost: $1.
- Professional Sports Hall of Fame, 8 miles south of Bandon on U.S. Highway 101. Cost: $2.
- West Coast Game Park Walk-Thru Safari, 7 miles south of Bandon on U.S. Highway 101. Cost: $5.95.
- Ripley's Believe It Or Not Museum, 250 Southwest Bay Boulevard, Newport. Cost: $5.
- Undersea Garden, 250 Southwest Bay Boulevard, Newport. Cost: $5.
- The Wax Works, 250 Southwest Bay Boulevard, Newport. Cost: $5.
- Yaquina Bay Lighthouse in Yaquina Bay State Park, Newport. Cost: 50 cents.
- The Oregon Coast Aquarium on Yaquina Bay in Newport. Cost: $7.

Special Splurges
- Enjoy the ambiance of the five-star Salishan Lodge at Gleneden Beach north of Newport. There are lots of things you can do for free—hiking along three miles of secluded beach, window shopping at the elegant shops or just plain people-watching. Then splurge on a meal in one of their three five-star restaurants. Cost: $100 and up for two.
- This same lodge, the Salishan, may be a place for you to stay as well, if only for one night. Cost: From $100 to $220 per night.

WASHINGTON

HONEYMOON NO. 2 — THE SAN JUAN ISLANDS — VICTORIA

Note: You can take a cruise of the San Juan Islands, with Pacific Northwest Cruises out of Seattle, on which you sleep and eat aboard the ship. Weekend cruises run about $299 per person; six-day cruises run about $699 per person. Call (206)441-8687. Otherwise, I am assuming you will take a state ferry to each of the ports listed below. This will run about $35 per person per port and you will need to book a motel or hotel at each of your destinations.

Route
- Depart for the San Juan Islands from Anacortes, Washington (about 85 miles north of Seattle) on a Washington State ferry. The fares vary according to the number of destination ports, but a sample fare would be from Anacortes to Orcas Island and back. This round-trip fare would include $16 for your car, plus about $5 per person, for a total of $36. Call (206)464-6400 for rates and times of departure. Suggested destination ports: Friday Harbor, Port Townsend and Victoria.

Romantic Appeal

- The fun of cruising, although via a state ferry.
- The allure of the scenic ports.
- Victoria's British ambiance, including double-decker buses, horse-drawn carriages and profuse English gardens.

Free Attractions

- Whale-watching; also, watch for bald eagles, great horned owls, seals and dolphins.
- Swimming, hiking, beachcombing and people-watching.
- Walking tours of Anacortes, Friday Harbor, Port Townsend and Victoria.
- Hike around Bastion Square, overlooking the harbor at Victoria.
- Attend a recital at The Netherlands Centennial Carillon in Heritage Court. One-hour recitals are performed every Sunday at 3 P.M. all year, and on Wednesdays at noon and Fridays at 6 P.M. from July 1 through September 16.
- Fort Worden State Park, 1 mile north of Port Townsend offers 341 acres of hiking, plus performing arts presentations from mid-June to early September.
- Jefferson County Historical Museum, Madison and Water streets, Port Townsend.
- Rothschild House, Franklin and Taylor streets, Port Townsend.

Low-Cost Attractions

- Scuba diving, fishing, bicycling and sightseeing.
- While in Victoria, take a scenic drive along highways 17 and 17A to Butchart Gardens, a "must-see" on any Victorian visit. Cost: $10.17 per person (this includes the fireworks displays on Saturday evenings in July and August).
- Collectors' Car Museum, 813 Douglas Street in Victoria. Cost: $5.
- Craigdarroch Castle, 1050 Joan Crescent Street, Victoria. Cost: $4.
- Fable Cottage Estate and World Class Gardens, 5187 Cordova Bay Road off Highway 17. Cost: $7.50.
- Sealand on Beach Drive, Victoria. Cost: $6.50.
- Harbour Tours of Victoria. Cost: $6 to $9.
- Dancing at the Old Forge, 919 Douglas Street, Victoria, or at the Strathcona Hotel, downtown Victoria. Cost: Approximately $25 per couple.

Special Splurges

- Have high tea at the Tudor Room of the Oak Bay Beach Hotel in Victoria. Cost: $25 to $30 per person.
- Eat and stay at States Inn, Friday Harbor, an historic bed-and-breakfast on a working ranch in a pastoral valley. Cost: $80 to $95 per night.

HONEYMOON NO. 3 — SEATTLE

Romantic Appeal

- The excitement of a big city.
- The scenery, including mountain views and water, water, water.
- The water lends itself to sensual cruises and ferry rides.

Free Attractions

- Free bus service within the downtown area. For route information, call (206)553-3000.
- Discovery Park (at West Government Way and Thirty-sixth Avenue West) offers 2 miles of beach, nature trails and the West Point Light Station (accessible by a 1½ mile hike).
- Fishermen's Terminal (off Fifteenth Avenue West at 1735 West Thurman Street). This harbor is the home port to the fishing fleet and has a wonderful waterfront plaza.
- Klondike Gold Rush Historical Park (in Pioneer Square at 117 South Main Street).
- Walking tours of Chinatown or Pioneer Square Historic District.
- If you're in Seattle from mid-July to early August, enjoy the entertainment available at the 23-day Seattle Seafair, including parades and hydroplane races on Lake Washington.

Low-Cost Attractions

- Take a one-hour Seattle Harbor Tours trip on which you will see Seattle from the water. Purchase tickets at Pier 55. Call (206)623-1445. Cost: $8.50.
- Take a 2¼-hour sightseeing tour of the Seattle waterfront, the Lake Washington Ship Canal, and the Hirman Chittenden Locks on a Gray Line Water Tour. Call (206)623-4252. Cost: $18.
- Museum of Flight (½ mile northwest of I-5 exit 158 at 9404 East Marginal Way South). Cost: $5.
- Omnidome Film Experience at Pier 59 shows the film *The Eruption of Mount St. Helens*. Cost: $5.95.
- Seattle Aquarium, 1483 Alaskan Way. Cost: $5.75.
- Space Needle, 1 mile from downtown near Elliott Bay. Cost: $4.75 for the elevator ride to the top (605-feet high). If you purchase breakfast, the elevator ride is free.
- Bill Speidel Underground Tour (the five-block area under Pioneer Square). The tour departs from Doc Maynard's Public House in the Pioneer Building at First and James streets. Cost: $4.75.
- For the cost of a couple of drinks, enjoy entertainment at these spots: the Garden Court at the Four Seasons Hotel; the Lobby Bar at the Westin; the Cloud Room at Camlin Hotel; the Visions Lounge at Stouffer-Madisons; The Backstage; The Owl Cafe; Old Timer's Cafe; Dimitriou's Jazz Alley; Comedy Underground; and Giggles.

Special Splurges
- Blake Island Marine State Park, accessible only by boat. Cost: $18.45.
- Spirit of Puget Sound cruise (Pier 70 on Alaskan Way at the foot of Broad Steet). They offer four cruises:

  Lunch cruise (except Saturday)   Cost: $19.35 per person
  Brunch and Saturday lunch   Cost: $21.40 per person
  Dinner cruise   Cost: $36 to $41 per person
  Moonlight party cruise   Cost: $14 per person
- Dinner at Canlis, 2576 Aurora Avenue North (overlooks Lake Union and the Cascades). Outstanding view. Cost: Entrees start at about $25.

IDAHO
HONEYMOON NO. 4 — SUN VALLEY

Route
- Highway 75 north of Twin Falls to Sun Valley.

Romantic Appeal
- The amorous aura of Sun Valley, one of the most popular year-round resorts in the world; the resort resembles a European alpine village.
- The sensuality of a sleigh ride in winter or a summer concert under the stars.

Free Attractions
- Shoshone Falls, known as the Niagara of the West, 5 miles northeast of Twin Falls.
- The Herrett Museum, 315 Falls Avenue, Twin Falls.
- Hiking, sightseeing and shopping at Sun Valley.
- Free outdoor concerts at Sun Valley.
- Twenty art galleries at Sun Valley.
- Major events throughout the year at Sun Valley, including: January — Celebrity Invitational Cup, July through late August — Sun Valley Music Festival, Mid-August — Summerdance and the Sun Valley Center Arts and Crafts Fair, Labor Day weekend — Wagon Days, Mid-September — Oktoberfest, and Mid-October — Swing n' Dixie Jazz Jamboree.

Low-Cost Attractions
- Enjoy lunch on the patio at Christiania Restaurant on Sun Valley Road in Ketchum. Cost: $11 to $20 per person.
- Shoshone Ice Caves, on Highway 75 on the way to Sun Valley. Cost: $4.50.

Special Splurges

- High Adventure River Tour offers float trips on the Snake River. Cost: $45 to $75, depending on the trip length and whether meals are included. Call (208)733-0123.
- Stay at Sun Valley's Elkhorn Resort. Cost: Two people/one bed starting at $58 in the summer and $88 in the winter.
- Eat at least one meal at the pricey Sun Valley Lodge Dining Room. After dinner: dancing and entertainment. Cost: Entrees start at about $30 per person.

CHAPTER 10

THE LAND OF SEDUCTIVE SAND DUNES
Affordable Honeymoons in the Great Southwest
Arizona, New Mexico, Utah and Nevada

ARIZONA
HONEYMOON NO. 1 — TUCSON

Route
- Highway I-10 south out of Phoenix to Tucson, or
- Highway I-8 west out of Yuma to I-10 and
- Highway I-10 south to Tucson.

Romantic Appeal
- Nature's own painted deserts contrasted with the high mountain peaks.
- Sunsets to hug by.

Free Attractions
- Arizona Historical Museum, 949 East Second Street.
- Kitt Peak National Observatory, 56 miles southwest off State Route 86 in the Quinlan Mountains of the Sonoran Desert.
- Mission San Xavier, 9 miles southwest on San Xavier Road in the Tohono O'Odham Indian Reservation.
- Sentinel Peak Park off Broadway, west of I-10 on Cuesto (go at night for a fantastic view of Tucson's city lights).
- Walking tour of Tucson (pick up a walking tour map at the Metropolitan Tucson Convention Bureau at 130 South Scott Street).
- Hiking in Tucson Mountain Park and the Santa Catalina Mountains.

Low-Cost Attractions
- Arizona-Sonora Desert Museum, 14 miles west in Tucson Mountain Park. Cost: $6.
- The Breakers Waterpark, nine miles north to Exit I-10, then east 1½ miles at 8555 West Tangerine Road. Cost: $7.95.
- Colossal Cave, 20 miles southeast, then 6 miles north of I-10. Cost: $5.50.
- International Wildlife Museum, 7 miles west via Speedway Boulevard and West Gates Pass Road. Cost: $4.
- Old Tucson Studios, 12 miles west via Speedway Boulevard in Tucson Mountain Park. Cost: $9.95.

- Tucson Museum of Art, 140 North Main Street. Cost: $2.
- The Moonlight Shuttle to Upper Sabino Canyon after dark. Cost: $5.
- For the cost of drinks only you can dance at Larry Colligan's Hidden Valley Inn at 4825 North Sabino Canyon Road, The Baron's at 2401 South Wilmot Road, and the Flying V in Loews Ventana Canyon Resort.

Special Splurges

- The Last Territory steak house and live music at the Sheraton Tucson El Conquistador Hotel, 10,000 North Oracle Road. Cost: About $20 per person, includes free musical entertainment and Old West theme.
- If you can afford it, try to stay at least one night at either Loews Ventana Canyon Resort or Sheraton Tucson El Conquistador. Cost: Ranges from about $100 for two people/one bed in the summer to $250 the rest of the year.

HONEYMOON NO. 2 — FLAGSTAFF — SEDONA

Route

- Highway 17 north out of Phoenix to Highway 179.
- Highway 179 northwest off Highway 17 to Sedona.
- Highway 99 north out of Sedona to Flagstaff.
- Highway 17 south out of Flagstaff to Phoenix.

Romantic Appeal

- The fascination of Sedona, the artists' mecca.
- The refreshing whisper of the wind as it blows through Flagstaff's evergreen trees.

Free Attractions

- Walking tour of Sedona, including its art galleries; walking tour of Flagstaff.
- Take a scenic drive through the Sedona Red Rocks area.
- Sedona Arts Center, north on U.S. 89A at Art Barn Road.
- Scenic drive through Schultz Pass between the San Francisco Peaks and the Elden Mountains. Take Schultz Pass Road.
- Lowell Observatory, one mile west of Flagstaff via Santa Fe Avenue on Mars Hill. The one-hour tour includes the chance to look through the gigantic telescope.

Low-Cost Attractions

- Museum of Northern Arizona, 3 miles north on U.S. 180. Cost: $4.
- Riordan State Historic Park, 1 mile south via Milton Road at 1300 Riordan Ranch Street. Cost: $2.

- Snow Bowl, 15 miles northwest on Fort Valley Road in the San Francisco Peaks. Take the chairlift to 11,500 feet for a view of the Grand Canyon. Cost: $7.

Special Splurges
- Hot-air balloon ride over the Sedona and Oak Creek Canyon. The balloon leaves at sunrise, includes a champagne picnic, and returns about 9 A.M. Cost: $135 per person.
- Dinner at L'Auberge de Sedona Restaurant at L'Auberge de Sedona Resort, one block north of highways 89A and 179. Elegant French dining with six-course meals. Cost: About $100 for two people.
- Stay at least one night at the Hillside at L'Auberge Motor Inn on Highway 89A overlooking Oak Creek Canyon. Cost: Two people/one bed starts at about $100 per night.

NEW MEXICO

HONEYMOON No. 3 — SANTA FE — TAOS

Route
- Highway 25 north out of Albuquerque to Highway 285.
- Highway 285 north off Highway 25 to Santa Fe.
- Highway 285 north out of Santa Fe to Highway 68.
- Highway 68 north to Taos.

Romantic Appeal
- You'll think you're in Barcelona, Spain, as you walk hand in hand through Santa Fe.
- The intrigue and fascination of Taos, home of many world-renowned artists.
- The sensuality of the food. Restaurants abound.

Free Attractions
- Walking tours of Santa Fe and Taos.
- Cathedral of St. Francis of Assisi, one block east of the Plaza in Santa Fe.
- Contemporary Arts Center, 291 East Barcelona Road, Santa Fe.
- Cristo Rey Church, Canyon Road and Camino Cabra in Santa Fe.
- American Indian Arts Museum, 1369 Cerrillos Road, in Santa Fe.
- Mission of San Miguel of Santa Fe, three blocks south of the Plaza in Santa Fe.
- Mission of the Pueblo of Tesuque, 8 miles north of Santa Fe.
- Museum of Fine Arts across from the Palace of Governors in Santa Fe.
- Museum of Indian Arts and Culture, off the Old Santa Fe Trail at 710 Camino Lejo in Santa Fe.
- Museum of International Folk Art, 706 Camino Lejo in Santa Fe.
- Palace of the Governors, north side of the Plaza in Santa Fe.

Low-Cost Attractions

- Footsteps Across New Mexico, 211 Old Santa Fe Trail, Santa Fe. Cost: $3.50.
- Museum of New Mexico in Santa Fe. Cost: $3.50.
- Ernest Blumenschein Home, two blocks east of Taos Plaza in Taos. Ernest Blumenschein was an artist and cofounder of the original Taos Society of Artists. This adobe building, dating back to 1790, presently serves as a showcase for the paintings of various Taos artists. Cost: $3.
- Kit Carson Home and Museum, a half block east of Taos Plaza in Taos. Cost: $3.
- Martinez Hacienda, 2 miles west of Taos Plaza on Ranchitos Road, built in 1804 by Martinez, mayor of Taos. Coast: $3.
- Taos Pueblo, 2½ miles north of Taos Plaza. Cost: $5 for parking, $4 for bringing a still camera, and $10 for bringing a movie or video camera.

Special Splurges

- Take a raft trip on the Rio Grande. Contact Far Flung Adventures (505)758-2628. Cost: $38 to $150 per person.
- Stay at least one night at Hotel Santa Fe, four blocks southwest of the Plaza. Cost: Two people/one bed, from $110 to $190 per night.

HONEYMOON NO. 4 — CARLSBAD

Route

- Highway 285 south out of Roswell to Carlsbad.

Romantic Appeal

- For the adventurous couple, the chill of the stalagmites and stalactites, the thrill of bats in flight, the still of the darkness as you hold hands in New Cave.
- More adventure at President's Park amusement park in Carlsbad.

Free Attractions

- Carlsbad Museum and Art Center on Fox Street, Carlsbad.
- Walking tours of Carlsbad and Roswell.
- Hike through the Bitter Lake National Wildlife Refuge, 10 miles northeast of Roswell off Highway 70/285.
- Spring River Park and Zoo, 1 mile north on College Boulevard in Roswell.
- Roswell Museum and Art Center, Eleventh and Main streets, Roswell.

Low-Cost Attractions

- Living Desert State Park, 4 miles northwest on Highway 285 out of Carlsbad. Cost: $3.
- Carlsbad Caverns National Park. Cost: $5.

- Stay at least one night at the Best Western Sally Port Inn in Roswell. It has a heated indoor pool, whirlpool, lighted tennis court and indoor recreation area. Cost: Two people/one bed, about $65 per night.

Special Splurges
- President's Park, an amusement park at Lake Carlsbad in the center of the town of Carlsbad. Cost: About $50 per couple for a full day's entertainment, including a 1903 carousel and a sternwheeler ride up the river.

UTAH

Honeymoon No. 5 — Salt Lake City — Logan — Bear Lake

Route
- Highway 80 from the east or west to Salt Lake City.
- Highway 89 north out of Salt Lake City to Logan and Bear Lake.

Romantic Appeal
- The perfect combination of city and country, each with its own emotional stir.
- Snuggle under a bear rug on a sleigh ride in the winter.

Free Attractions
- Walking tour of historical Salt Lake City, including South Temple Street with its nineteenth-century architecture, the Eagle Gate, the Brigham Young Monument, the Family History Library, the Salt Palace, the Delta Center, the First Presbyterian Church, the Exchange Place Historic District, and the Marmalade Historic District.
- Hiking along Canyon Road in City Creek Canyon, Salt Lake City.
- Beehive House, 67 East South Temple Street, Salt Lake City.
- Cathedral of the Madeleine, 331 East South Temple Street, Salt Lake City.
- Liberty Park, 500 East Street, Salt Lake City.
- Pioneer Trail State Park, at the mouth of Emigration Canyon, east of Salt Lake City.
- Free organ recitals at the Tabernacle, North Temple Street, Salt Lake City. Weekdays at noon and weekends at 4 P.M.
- Harrison Museum of Art on the Utah State University campus at 650 North 1100 East Street in Logan.
- Hardware Ranch, 17 miles southeast of Logan. Free sleigh rides in the winter to view and photograph the elk.
- Hike and swim at Bear Lake.

Low-Cost Attractions

- Hansen Planetarium, 15 South State Street, Salt Lake City. Cost: $5.50.
- Hogle Zoological Gardens, 2600 East Sunnyside Avenue, Salt Lake City. Cost: $4.
- Raging Waters, 1200 West 1700 South, a 17-acre water theme park, Salt Lake City. Cost: $11.95.
- Ronald Jensen Living Historical Farm, 6 miles south on Highway 89 out of Logan. Cost. $2.

Special Splurges

- Stay at least one night at the Center Street Bed and Breakfast in Logan. Cost: Two people/one bed, about $75 per night.
- Enjoy a meal at Ninos on the twenty-fourth floor of the University Club, 136 East South Temple Place, Salt Lake City. Very "pricey," but the panoramic view is thrown in for free. Go for lunch instead of dinner and you will save about half. Cost: $60 to $75 per couple.
- If you can afford it, try to stay one night at the Pinecrest Bed & Breakfast Inn, 6211 Emigration Canyon Road in Salt Lake City. Cost: Two people/one bed, about $125 per night.

NEVADA

HONEYMOON NO. 6 — CARSON CITY — VIRGINIA CITY — LAKE TAHOE

Route

- Highway 395 south out of Reno to Carson City.
- Highway 50 northeast out of Carson City to Highway 341.
- Highway 341 north of Highway 50 to Virginia City.
- Retrace route back to Carson City.
- Highway 50 west out of Carson City to South Shore, Lake Tahoe.

Romantic Appeal

- From the Old West to the glamour of the country's most beautiful lake, this is a delightful honeymoon trip.
- Get grubby together as you hike around the ghost towns.
- Snuggle up as the wind whips up on your Lake Tahoe cruise.
- Get glamorous together as you enjoy the nightlife of South Shore.

Free Attractions

- Walking tours of Carson City, Virginia City and Bodie.

- State Museum, 600 North Carson Street, Carson City.
- Stewart Indian Museum, 5366 Snyder Avenue, Carson City.
- Mark Twain Museum of Memories, C and Taylor streets, Virginia City.
- Nevada Fire Museum, 51 South C Street, Virginia City.
- Hike along the beaches of South Shore, Lake Tahoe.

Low-Cost Attractions

- Take a side trip north of Carson City on Highway 395 to the actual Ponderosa Ranch featured on the ''Bonanza'' television show. It is now a theme park with a saloon, museum, mystery mine, etc. Cost: Admittance only, $7.50 per person; breakfast hay ride, $9.50 per person.
- A cruise around Lake Tahoe on the M.S. *Dixie*, leaving from Zephyr Cove and South Shore. Cost: $14.
- Bowers Mansion Park, 10 miles north of Carson City on Highway 395. Cost: $1.
- Nevada State Railroad Museum, 2180 South Carson Street, Carson City. Cost: $2.50, which includes the train ride.
- A side trip south to Bodie State Historic Park (in California) 20 miles southeast of Bridgeport, California, via Highway 395. This is an old gold-mining town. Cost: $5 per car.
- The Castle, 70 South B Street, Virginia City. Cost: $2.75.
- Chollar Mine, South F Street, Virginia City. Cost: $4.
- Mackay Mansion, 129 D Street, Virginia City. Cost: $3.
- Virginia and Truckee Railroad, 35-minute train ride between Virginia City and Gold Hill. Cost: $4, round-trip fare.

Special Splurges

- Dinner at the top of Harvey's Casino on the Nevada side of South Shore, Lake Tahoe. I give the view, cuisine and service five stars! Cost: $80 to $100 for two people.
- Take in a show at Harrah's, The Horizon or Caesar's. Cost: About $26 per person.

CHAPTER 11

THE LAND OF THE FLIRTY TWO-STEP
Affordable Texas Honeymoons

HONEYMOON NO. 1 — SAN ANTONIO

Route

- Highway 35 south out of Fort Worth to San Antonio, or
- Highway 10 west out of El Paso to San Antonio, or
- Highway 10 east out of Houston to San Antonio.

Romantic Appeal

- San Antonio has been called a "Mexican Disneyland for adults," and it certainly lives up to its reputation.
- Mild weather year-round; perfect for honeymooners who love to "go-see-do" about town.
- San Antonio has a festive atmosphere, just right for honeymooners who are already in a good mood.

Free Attractions

- The Alamo, downtown near the river.
- Fort Sam Houston, between Highway 35 and Harry Wurzbach Highway.
- Hemisfair Plaza, bounded by Commerce, Market, Durango and Alamo streets, offers free daily entertainment. The San Antonio River runs through the center of the plaza.
- Market Square, bounded by Dolorosa, Santa Rosa and West Commerce streets, offers artists' works, a farmers' market, specialty shops and food galleries. This is also where the special celebrations take place, including Cinco de Mayo in May and Fiestas de Navidenas in December.
- The Riverwalk (Paseo Del Rio) is a prime attraction; it provides tree-lined footpaths perfect for lovers. You can dine, shop or just people-watch.
- Mission Trail includes a tour of four missions. Pick up a free driving map at the San Antonio Visitor Information Center, 317 Alama Park.

Low-Cost Attractions

- Steves Homestead, 509 King William Street. Cost: $2.
- Brackenridge Park, 3903 North St. Mary's Street, includes lagoons, a miniature railroad, horseback riding, paddle boats, oriental gardens, a skyride to the zoo, etc. Cost: Skyride,

$4; Zoo, $5.

- Imax Theatre, in the RiverCenter Mall downtown, presents a film that recounts the battle of the Alamo. Cost: $5.75.
- Malibu Castle, 3330 Cherry Ridge Drive, is an amusement park that includes a miniature golf course, bumper boats, etc. Cost: $3 to $5.50 per amusement.
- Ripley's Believe It or Not! at 301 Alamo Plaza has 225 wax figures. Cost: $5.45.
- Try out that two-step at any number of night spots for the cost of a one- or two-drink minimum or a reasonable cover charge. The Farmer's Daughter, 542 Northwest White, will even teach you western dance steps, in case you're beginners. Also, try the Beauregard for rock, polka and swing, Jim Cullum's (at the Hyatt Regency Hotel) for Dixieland and the Roaring '20s for big band sounds.
- San Antonio Botanical Gardens, 555 Funston Place. Cost: $3.
- Splashtown, on Coliseum Road off Highway 35N at exit 160, includes waterslides and other amusements. Cost: $12.95.
- Boat tours down the San Antonio River. Cost: Starts at $1.75 per person.

Special Splurges
- Sea World of Texas, 10,500 Sea World Drive. Cost: $20.95.
- Stay at least one night at La Mansion del Rio, right on the San Antonio River. Cost: Two people/one bed, about $150 per night.
- Eat lunch at the River Grill in the Marriott Rivercenter. Cost: About $50 for two.

Honeymoon No. 2 — Corpus Christi — Padre Seashore — Mustang Island

Route
- Highway 37 south out of San Antonio to Corpus Christi.
- Highway 358 out of Corpus Christi to Mustang Island.
- Laguna Madre Causeway south from Mustang Island to Padre National Seashore.

Romantic Appeal
- Water is very sensual, and Corpus Christi has plenty of it, from its own freshwater lake (Lake Corpus Christi), to Corpus Christi Bay, to the beaches of Padre and Mustang Islands.
- Less to see and do than in San Antonio; more privacy and seclusion where you can escape reality and experience the moment.

Free Attractions

- Walks along Corpus Christi Bay; take the stairs that lead from downtown to the water.
- Free festivals throughout the year, including Buccaneer Days in April, Bayfest in September, and the Texas Jazz Festival in July.
- Walking tour of Old Town Corpus Christi.
- Naturalist programs at the Malaquite Visitor Center on Padre Island.
- Walks along the beaches of Padre Island and Mustang Island.

Low-Cost Attractions

- Museum of Oriental Cultures, 418 Peoples Street. Cost: $1.
- Texas State Aquarium, 2710 North Shoreline Boulevard. Cost: $7.
- Corpus Christi Museum of Science and History, 1900 North Chaparral. Cost: $2.
- Padre Island National Seashore, 66 miles of the total 113 miles of Padre Island. Cost: $3 per car.

Special Splurges

- Enjoy a meal at Reflections in the Marriott Bayfront hotel, where you will have a view of the bay and the city. Cost: About $80 for two.
- If you can afford it, you might want to stay at least one night at this same hotel, the Corpus Christi Marriott Bayfront. The rooms have private balconies overlooking the bay. Cost: Two people/one bed, about $140 per night.

HONEYMOON NO. 3 — PORT ISABEL — HARLINGEN — SOUTH PADRE ISLAND

Route

- Highway 77 south out of Corpus Christi to Harlingen.
- Highway 77 south out of Harlingen to South Padre Island Road.
- South Padre Island Road east off of Highway 77 to Port Isabel and South Padre Island.

Romantic Appeal

- The alluring beach sands of South Padre Island, just right for the honeymooning couple.
- Massage the stress away with suntan lotion as you stretch out along the gulf water.

Free Attractions

- Bring along a metal detector and hunt for rumored buried treasure in the sands of South Padre Island.
- Beachcomb for rocks, shells, and debris washed ashore from old shipwrecks.
- Jog along the shoreline.
- Swim or body surf in the waves.

- Enjoy free entertainment during the Winter Park Blowout in May, the Texas International Fishing Tournament in August, or the Christmas by the Sea Festival in early December, all on South Padre Island.
- Rio Grande Valley Museum, Boxwood and Raintree streets, Harlingen.

Low-Cost Attractions

- Port Isabel Lighthouse State Historical Park, at Maxan and Tarnava streets, Port Isabel. Cost: $1.
- Water sports galore on South Padre Island, including jet skiing, diving, windsurfing, parasailing, sailing and board saling. Cost: Varies.
- Other sports available on South Padre Island: golf, racquetball, shuffleboard, horseback riding and tennis. Cost: Varies.

Special Splurges

- Stay a night or two, if you can afford it, at the Sheraton South Padre Island Beach Resort, which offers swimming (in a pool or in the gulf), tennis, whirlpool, and a nightclub with excellent live entertainment. Cost: Two people/one bed, about $100 to $130 per night.
- Try a meal at Scampi's on the bay, 3 miles north of Queen Isabella Causeway. Cost: $50 for two.

CHAPTER 12

The Land of the Snowcaps
Affordable Rocky Mountain Honeymoons
Colorado, Montana and Wyoming

COLORADO

Honeymoon No. 1 — Lake Dillon — Vail

Route
- Highway 70 west out of Denver to Lake Dillon and Vail.

Romantic Appeal
- This Alpine-style town, resting between the White River National Forest and 14,000-foot-high mountain peaks, is an internationally renowned resort center. It offers honeymooners a romantic interlude in a Tyrolean setting.

Free Attractions
- Hiking around Dillon Lake.
- Walking tour of Vail; including musical entertainment on the streets.
- Entertainment during Vail's festivals, including Vailfest in late September.
- Cross-country skiing in Keystone (near Lake Dillon) or at Vail, including night skiing.
- Ice skating in Keystone in the winter.
- Shop in Vail for fascinating imported goods, many quite affordable. Bring your Christmas list.
- People-watch on the streets of Vail; keep your eye out for celebrities, including the Kennedy clan who has a winter home in Vail.

Low-Cost Attractions
- Rent a bicycle for about $5 an hour.
- Go horseback riding at Keystone or in Vail. Cost: Starts at about $25.
- Colorado Ski Museum, Ski Hall of Fame, Vail. Cost: $1.
- Lionshead Gondola ride, Vail. Cost: $10.
- Gondola rides, Keystone. Cost: $8.
- Paddle-boating on Lake Dillon. Cost: Starts at about $4 an hour.

Special Splurges
- Downhill skiing in the winter at Vail or Beaver Creek (west of Vail). Cost: Starts at about $40 for an all-day lift ticket.

- Vail has its pricey hotels and restaurants, but fortunately it has a few very good ones that are affordable. Try the Vailglo Lodge on South Frontage Road at Lionshead in Vail. It has a definite "lodge" feeling, a year-round swimming pool, a spa pool, and most rooms have balconies. The staff pride themselves on their personal service and the cozy, intimate atmosphere. Cost: $64 to $198 per night, depending on the season; this includes continental breakfast.
- You need to have at least one meal at Alfredo's in the Westin Resort-Vail. Make reservations for a table with a mountain view. Cost: About $75 for two.

HONEYMOON NO. 2 — DURANGO — SILVERTON — TELLURIDE — OURAY

Route
- Highway 50 south out of Grand Junction to Montrose.
- Highway 550 south out of Montrose to Ouray, Silverton and Durango.
- Highways 82 and 145 west off Highway 50 to Telluride.

Romantic Appeal
- Walk hand in hand into the wild West of the 1800s, including the mining towns, narrow gauge trains, and the old home of Bat Masterson.

Free Attractions
- Walking tours of Durango, Silverton, Ouray and Telluride. Silverton is often used as a movie set because of its authentic Western town restoration.
- Take a side trip (36 miles west of Durango) to Mesa Verde National Park, one of the nation's major archaeological preserves. Dating back to 500 A.D., Indian cliff dwellings can be viewed from overlooks.
- Take a tour over the Million Dollar Highway, part of the San Juan Scenic Byway (leads north out of Ouray).
- Telluride is known for its festivals, including a summer jazz festival, bluegrass festival, chamber music festival, film festival, and the Telluride Hang Gliding Festival. It is also the home of a bank robbed by Butch Cassidy, who made off with $30,000.
- Take a couple of well-known hikes out of Telluride. One is the hike to Bridal Veil Falls and another is a dramatic canyon hike that begins at the edge of town and climbs 1,100 feet to Bear Creek Falls.

Low-Cost Attractions
- Diamond Circle Theater, 699 Main Avenue in the Strater Hotel, Durango, offers nineteenth-century melodramas and vaudeville shows. Cost: $9.

- San Juan County Museum, Green Street, Silverton. Cost: $1.50.
- San Miguel County Historical Museum, 317 North Fir Street in Telluride. Cost: $2.
- Here is one of the greatest bargains around: Swim and soak in the Ouray Hot Springs Pool. Cost: $4.
- Bachelor-Syracuse Mine, one mile north on Highway 550, then 1¼ mile east on county Route 14. Cost: $7.95.
- Box Canyon, within the city limits of Ouray. Cost: $1.25.
- Tin Lizzie Tours, departing from 331 Sixth Avenue in Ouray. Cost: $6.

Special Splurges

- A real "must" if you honeymoon to Durango between May and October is a ride on The Durango and Silverton Narrow Gauge Railroad. This old coal-burning locomotive runs through the mountains of the San Juan National Forest to Silverton. Reservations required. Call (303)247-2733. Cost: $37.14 per person for a round-trip.
- Take a half day river raft trip down the Animas River. Call Mountain Waters at (800)748-2507. Cost: $25 per person for a four-hour trip.
- How about a bobsled-like run down the 2,200-foot track at Purgatory-Durango Ski Resort and Alpine Slide, 25 miles north of Durango off Highway 550. Cost: $25 per person for a half day or $3.25 for a single ride.
- How about a jeep tour to an historical ghost town? Try Colorado West Jeep Tours and Rentals or the San Juan Scenic Jeep Tours, both orginating out of Ouray. Cost: About $60 for a full day or $30 for a half day.
- The Box Canyon Lodge and Hot Springs in Ouray offers affordable honeymoon lodging that is special. This lodge is secluded, yet within walking distance of shops and restaurants, and it offers outdoor mineral hot springs hot tubs. Ask about their honeymoon suite. Cost: Starts at about $44 per night.

MONTANA

HONEYMOON NO. 3 — KALISPELL — FLATHEAD LAKE — COLUMBIA FALLS — WHITEFISH

Route

- Highway 93 north out of Missoula to Flathead Lake, Kalispell and Whitefish.
- Highway 40 east out of Whitefish to Columbia Falls.

Romantic Appeal

- From freshwater lakes, to cascading waterfalls, to the Park Between the Mountains, honeymooners will commune with nature on this outdoorsy adventure.

Free Attractions

- Walking tours of Kalispell, Columbia Falls, Whitefish and Polson (at Flathead Lake).
- Hungry Horse Dam, 32 miles northeast of Kalispell offers guided tours.
- Hike around Flathead Lake.
- Polson-Flathead Historical Museum, 802 Main Street, Polson.
- Spend a day on the beach at Flathead Lake, swimming and soaking up the sun. How about a picnic purchased at the local deli?
- Cross-country skiing at Big Mountain near Whitefish.

Low-Cost Attractions

- Conrad Mansion National Historic Site Museum, Main and Fourth streets, Kalispell. Cost: $4.
- Far West Cruise Ship at Vistas Linda Dock on Flathead Lake offers 1½ hour cruises. Cost: $7.
- Big Sky Waterslide, two blocks west of highways 2 and 206, Columbia Falls. Cost: $9.50 or $6.50 for a half day. Miniature golf only, $4.50.
- Miracle of America Museum, 2 miles south of Polson on Highway 93. Cost: $1.
- *Port Polson Princess* offers narrated tours of Flathead Lake. Cost: $15 for a three-hour tour and $10 for a two-hour tour.
- Big Mountain Ski and Summer Resort, 8 miles north of Whitefish, offers gondola rides to the 6,770-foot summit of The Big Mountain (views of northwestern Montana and southern Canada). Cost: $9.

Special Splurges

- Take a half-day whitewater raft trip through the lower Flathead River. Trips depart from the Glacier Raft Company at Riverside Park at the bridge in Polson (south Flathead Lake). Cost: $27.
- Ski in the wintertime. Cost: Lift tickets start at about $29 for all day.
- You can probably afford more than one night at Cavanaugh's at Kalispell Center, 20 North Main Street, Kalispell. It offers a heated pool, sauna and whirlpools. Ask for a room with its own private hot tub and fireplace. Cost: Starts at $76 per night.
- Enjoy dinner at Fenders Restaurant, 4090 Highway 93, Kalispell. It has a country setting with a wonderful view of the Flathead Valley. Cost: About $50 for two.

WYOMING

HONEYMOON NO. 4—JACKSON HOLE

Route
- Highway 191 north out of Rock Springs to Highway 89.
- Highway 89 north to Jackson.

Romantic Appeal
- This honeymoon is the nature-lovers' delight with its rafting, hiking and horseback riding. You will try to capture the scenery on film, but the reality of the grandeur can only be experienced in the moment.

Free Attractions
- Walking tour of Jackson.
- Many festivals, including Old West Days on Memorial Day Weekend, Grand Teton Music Festival from June through August, and Jackson Hole Fall Arts Festival in October.
- Cross-country skiing and snowshoe hikes in the winter.
- National Fish Hatchery and Aquarium, 4 miles north of Jackson on Highway 89.
- All the "freebies" of Grand Teton National Park (presented in detail in chapter 28), including backpacking, hiking, fishing and climbing.
- People-watching in downtown Jackson.

Low-Cost Attractions
- Snake River Park whitewater raft trip down the Snake River Canyon, departs 12 miles south of Jackson on Highway 26/89. Cost: $21 per person.
- Jackson Hole Aerial Tram, 12 miles northwest of Jackson on Highway 390 in Teton Village. Cost: $13.
- Jackson Hole Museum, at 101 North Glenwood Avenue in Jackson. Cost: $2.
- National Elk Refuge, Elk Refuge Road. Take a sleigh ride to view the elk. Cost: $7.50.
- Snow King Chairlift and Alpine Slide, 400 East Snow King Avenue, Jackson. Cost: $5.
- Wildlife of the American West Art Museum, 110 North Center, Jackson. Cost: $2.
- Many of the low-cost glories of Grand Teton National Park (presented in detail in chapter 28), including boating, horseback riding, wagon ride with dinner included, snowmobiling, guided snowmobile trips and float trips.

Special Splurges
- Stay at least one night at Spring Creek Resort in Jackson, on a secluded mountaintop with a world-class view. Cost: Two people/one bed, starts at about $100 per night.
- Try the Strutting Grouse Restaurant. Cost: About $60 for two.

CHAPTER 13

THE LAND OF TRADITIONS

Affordable Northeastern Honeymoons

New York, New Jersey and Pennsylvania

NEW YORK

HONEYMOON NO. 1 — LAKE GEORGE — LAKE PLACID

Route

- Highway 87 north out of Schenectady to Lake George.
- Highway 87 north out of Lake George to Highway 73.
- Highway 73 northwest to Lake Placid.

Romantic Appeal

- Surround yourselves with the languid lakes and buoyant beauty of the Adirondacks, a great honeymoon escape.

Free Attractions

- Swim and hike at Lake George and Lake Placid.
- Hike the self-guided trail through the grounds of the John Brown Farm State Historic Site, on John Brown Road in the town of Lake Placid.
- Shop along the Million-Dollar-Half-a-Mile in the Lake George area, on Highway 9.

Low-Cost Attractions

- Lake George Steamboat Company, on Beach Road, offers one-hour cruises. Cost: $6.50.
- Lake Placid Boat Rides, Lake Placid Marina, 1 mile north on Mirror Lake Drive, also offers one-hour cruises. Cost: $10.45.
- Olympic Center, Main Street in Lake Placid. Take a self-guided auto tour of the complex. Cost: $15.

Special Splurges

- Take a dinner cruise on Shoreline Cruises, located on Lake George waterfront at 2 Kurasaka Lane. Cost: $29.95 per person or $11.50 for their midnight cruise.
- Stay at the Mirror Lake Inn, Lake Placid, where you can have a room overlooking Mirror Lake, plus two heated swimming pools, sauna, whirlpool, tennis, ice skating, and canoeing and boating. Cost: Two people/one bed, varies from $71 to $100 per night.
- Another treat would be a meal at the Mirror Lake Inn Dining Room, also overlooking

Mirror Lake. Their evening meals are served by candlelight and rate a 10 on the "Honeymoon Romance Meter." Cost: About $75 for two.

Note: See chapter 27 for a special feature on New York City.

HONEYMOON NO. 2 — NIAGARA FALLS

Route

- Highway 90 (the New York Thruway) west out of Syracuse to Buffalo.
- Highway 190 north out of Buffalo to Niagara Falls.

Romantic Appeal

- Niagara Falls is America's traditional honeymoon destination, and you can enjoy it, too.

Free Attractions

- Albright-Knox Art Gallery, Elmwood Avenue, Buffalo.
- Buffalo and Erie County Botanical Gardens, McKinley Parkway, Buffalo.
- Walking tour of Buffalo, including Main and North Pearl streets and Delaware Avenue. Depart from the Wilcox Mansion, 641 Delaware Avenue. (If you want a guided tour, the cost is $5 per person.)
- Hike through the 264-acre Tifft Nature Preserve, west on Highway 5 to the second Fuhrmann exit, then left on South Service Road.
- Climb to the top of City Hall at Niagara Square for a 28-story view of the city of Buffalo.
- Buffalo offers plenty of free entertainment during their festivals. The city goes crazy on St. Patrick's Day, and in June historic Allentown lights up for the Allentown Art Festival. Also, there is the Friendship Festival over the Fourth of July holiday, as well as the Taste of Buffalo festival.
- Niagara Reservation State Park at Prospect Point, Niagara Falls, U.S.A.

Low-Cost Attractions

- Miss Buffalo Charter Cruises conducts two-hour cruises of Buffalo Harbor. Departures are from Marine Drive and Erie Street. Cost: $7.
- Try the nightlife at spots like Garvey's, The Continental, The Jam Club, and most of the lounges at the major hotels. The Breakers Restaurant on the shore of Lake Erie, 325 Fuhrmann Boulevard, draws a large summertime crowd.
- Buffalo Zoo at Delaware Park on Iroquois Drive. Cost: $3.
- Fantasy Island, north of Buffalo on Highway 190, exit 19N. Cost: $15.95.
- Aquarium of Niagara Falls, U.S.A., Whirlpool Street at Pine Avenue. Cost: $5.85.
- Cave of the Winds trip on Goat Island. Cost: $3.50.
- Maid of the Mist boats will take you directly in front of Niagara Falls. They leave from

the dock at Prospect Point on the American side of the Falls. Cost: $6.75.
- Niagara Splash Water Park, 700 Rainbow Boulevard, in Niagara Falls, U.S.A. Cost: $11.95.
- Marineland, 7657 Portage Road, Niagara Falls, Ontario. Cost: $14.95 to $17.95, depending on the time of year.
- Niagara Falls Imax Theatre, 6170 Buchanan Avenue, Niagara Falls, Ontario. Cost: $6.50.

Special Splurges
- Stay at least one night at Michael's Inn-by-the-Falls in Niagara Falls, Ontario. Ask for a room with a heart-shaped tub-for-two and a view of Niagara Falls. Cost: Two people/one bed, from $50 to $150 per night.
- Have lunch at Victoria Park Restaurant, Niagara Parkway at River Road in Niagara Falls, Ontario. It has an open-air balcony that overlooks the Falls. Cost: About $50 for two.

NEW JERSEY
HONEYMOON NO. 3 — CAPE MAY — OCEAN CITY

Route
- Garden State Parkway (a toll road) out of Atlantic City to Ocean City and Cape May.

Romantic Appeal
- Capturing the old-world, gingerbread romance of the Victorian era, this honeymoon combines beachcombing and buggy rides.

Free Attractions
- Walking tours of Cape May, Cape May Court House and Ocean City.
- Comb the beaches for Cape May Diamonds (quartz).
- Enjoy all the free entertainment during Cape May's many festivals, including The Tulip Festival in late April, the Cape May Music Festival in June and the Victorian Week Festival, which begins on Columbus Day.
- Enjoy free entertainment in Ocean City during their festivals, including The Night in Venice Boat Parade in July, the Miss Crustacean Hermit Crab Beauty Pageant in August, and the World's Championship Hermit Tree Crab Race, also in August. If you're honeymooning over Columbus Day, you won't want to miss their Indian Summer Weekend.
- Ocean City Historical Museum, Seventeenth and Simpson streets.

Low-Cost Attractions
- The John Holmes House Historical Museum in Cape May Court House. Cost: $2.
- Historic Cold Spring Village, 735 Seashore Road, Cape May, has 20 restored buildings, plus craft shops and exhibits. Cost: $1.50. Horse and buggy rides are $3 per person and Saturday night concerts are free.

Special Splurges

- Have a room overlooking the ocean if you can. Try to stay at the Beach Club Hotel at 1280 Boardwalk in Ocean City. Cost: Two people/one bed, about $100 per night.
- Try dinner at The Washington Inn, 801 Washington Street in Cape May. This Inn is an 1848 colonial plantation home and takes pride in its wine collection. Cost: About $60 for two.

PENNSYLVANIA

HONEYMOON NO. 4 — THE POCONOS

Route

- Highway 33 north out of Bethlehem to Highway 611
- Highway 611 northwest to Mt. Pocono.

Romantic Appeal

- A Pocono honeymoon is the synonym for "romance."

Free Attractions

- Pocono Knob, located ¼ mile south on Highway 611, then east on Knob Hill Road. This scenic overlook is one of the most famous views on the East Coast.
- Hike around the many lakes and waterfalls in the Pocono Mountains.
- Ice skate for free on the frozen lakes in the winter.

Low-Cost Attractions

- Pennsylvania Dutch Farm, 1 mile south of Mt. Pocono on Highway 611 and then east on Grange Road. Cost: $3.50.
- Pocono Adventures on Mules, 1 mile south of Mt. Pocono on Highway 611 at Mount Airy Lodge. Enjoy a mule ride into the back country. Cost: 45-minute ride—$15 per person; two-hour ride—$25 per person.
- Bushkill Falls, 2 miles northwest of Bushkill off Highway 209. Not only are there eight waterfalls, but virgin forests, scenic bridges and a wildlife exhibit. Cost: $4.50.
- Pocono Indian Museum, 3 miles south of Bushkill on Highway 209. Cost: $3.
- Camelback Alpine Slide and Waterslide, Tannersville, 3½ miles northwest of Highway 80 at exit 45. Cost: $5.

Special Splurges

- Whitewater Challengers Raft Tours, White Haven, Pennsylvania, 6 miles south of Highway 80 at exit 40, just off Weatherly-White Haven Road. Take a three- to five-hour raft trip down the Lehigh River. Cost: Winter—$44 per person; Summer—$29 per person.
- The Great Eastern Balloon Association, Shawnee on Delaware. Cost: $165 per person.

- Have dinner at Hampton Court Inn Restaurant, Mt. Pocono on Highway 940. Cost: About $50 for two.

Honeymoon No. 5 — The Pennsylvania Dutch Country

Route

- Highway 30 west out of Philadelphia to Lancaster.

Romantic Appeal

- Become romantic "actors" on an authentic Amish movie set as you picnic along the "old mill stream" or ride in a horse-drawn carriage.

Free Attractions

- Heritage Center Museum of Lancaster, Penn Square in Lancaster.
- Lancaster County Historical Society, Rawlinsville Road in Lancaster.
- Lancaster Newspapers Newseum, 28 South Queen Street, Lancaster.

Low-Cost Attractions

- The Amish Homestead, 3 miles east of Lancaster on Highway 462. Cost: $4.
- The Amish Farm and House, 5 miles east of Lancaster on Highway 30. Cost. $4.25.
- Dutch Wonderland, 4 miles east of Lancaster on Highway 30, is an amusement park and garden. Cost: $10.50 (includes five rides).
- Lancaster Walking Tour, departing from Queen and Vine streets. Cost: $4.
- Landis Valley Museum, 2½ miles north of Lancaster on Oregon Pike. Cost: $5.
- Mill Bridge Village, 4 miles east of Lancaster at the junction of highways 30 and 462. This is a restored colonial village that has working craftsmen, a covered bridge, and an old-fashioned gazebo. Entertainment is provided on some weekends, along with horse-drawn carriage rides. Cost: $10 per person.
- National Wax Museum of Lancaster County Heritage, 4 miles east of Lancaster on Highway 30. Cost: $4.25.

Special Splurges

- Reserve at least one night at the Lancaster Host Resort at 2300 Lincoln Highway East, Lancaster. The resort offers many amenities including swimming pools, golf, movies, sauna, bicycles and tennis. Cost: Two people/one bed, about $100 per night.
- Be sure to have Sunday brunch at the elegant Windows on Steinman Park off Center Square in Lancaster. Cost: About $60 for two.

CHAPTER 14

THE LAND OF COLONIAL CHARISMA
Affordable New England Honeymoons
Massachusetts, Connecticut, Vermont, New Hampshire, Maine and Rhode Island

MASSACHUSETTS
HONEYMOON NO. 1 — BOSTON

Romantic Appeal

- Boston is a great "go-see-do" honeymoon city. From Harborwalk to the Boston Tea Party ship, your days will be full as you explore Boston together.

Free Attractions

- Walking tours of Boston called Boston By Foot; there are six to choose from, including the Freedom Trail Walking Tour.
- Park Street Church, Park and Tremont streets.
- Old North Church, 193 Salem Street.
- Hikes along the Charles and Mystic rivers.
- Rub shoulders with the rich and famous as you window-shop at Copley Place, which features Gucci's, Neiman-Marcus and Yves Saint Laurent.
- You may actually be able to buy something at Quincy Market, another fun place to shop. Vendors even offer their wares in pushcarts along the market streets.
- If you're in Boston over the Fourth of July, attend the free Boston Pops Orchestra concert at Hatch Memorial Shell on the Charles River.
- There is never a lack of entertainment in and around this city, especially during their annual celebrations. On December 15 there is a reenactment of The Boston Tea Party; on June 17 there is The Battle of Bunker Hill Celebration; The Boston Marathon, of course, is held on the third Monday of April; The Head of the Charles Regatta, a sculling event, draws thousands of spectators to the banks of the Charles River on the third Sunday of October; Boston's First Night, held every New Year's Eve, features more than 100 arts and entertainment groups.

Low-Cost Attractions

- The Boston Tea Party Ship and Museum at Congress Street Bridge. Cost: $6.
- The Boston subway is not only a tourist attraction, but is a very inexpensive, practical way to get around Boston. You will want to park your car somewhere and ride the subway or walk to all your destinations because Boston is definitely not a user-friendly

city when it comes to its street layout. You can purchase a three- or seven-day Boston Passport for unlimited subway passage. Cost: The three-day Boston Passport costs $9 and the seven-day pass $18. Otherwise, you will pay 85 cents per fare within the city.

- Bay State Cruises offers narrated trips to Fort Warren on Georges Island in Boston Harbor Islands State Park. Cost: Round-trip ticket—$5.
- Tour Gibson House Museum, 137 Beacon Street. Cost: $3.
- Harrison Otis House, 141 Cambridge Street. Otis was a lawyer, entrepreneur and Boston's third mayor. Cost: $4.
- Institute of Contemporary Art, 955 Boylston Street. Cost: $4.
- Isabella Stewart Gardner Museum, 280 Fenway. Cost: $6.
- John Hancock Observatory, the highest vantage point in New England, has a view of the city and suburbs. Cost: $2.75.
- The Museum at the John Fitzgerald Kennedy Library, on the campus of the University of Massachusetts, exit 14 off Highway 93. Cost: $4.50.
- Museum of Fine Arts, 465 Huntington Avenue. Cost: $6.
- Museum of Science at Science Park. Cost: $6.
- New England Aquarium at Central Wharf off Atlantic Avenue. Cost: $7.50.
- Nichols House Museum, 55 Mt. Vernon Street. This Federal-style house, in Beacon Hill, was the home of Rose Standish Nichols, a prominent Bostonian. Cost: $3.
- Paul Revere House, 19 North Square. Cost: $2.
- Prudential Center Tower Skywalk (between Huntington Avenue and Boylston Street). Cost: $2.75.
- A Swan Boat ride at Public Garden, bounded by Boylston, Charles, Beacon and Arlington streets. Cost: 95 cents.
- *Whites of Their Eyes*, a play performed in the Bunker Hill Pavilion. Cost: $3.

Special Splurges

- Finding a nice yet affordable hotel in Boston isn't easy, although Howard Johnson's has two hotels that run about $80 per night; also, you may want to consider the Boston Park Plaza Hotel on Arlington Street at Park Plaza which advertises a rate of "$53 per person, per night, subject to availability." This isn't bad at all for what you get; it includes free breakfast every day, as well as in-room movies, an exercise room, and evening entertainment in their nightclub.
- For a giant splurge, why not put on your best duds and enjoy Sunday brunch at either the Aujourd'hui in the Four Seasons Hotel (which overlooks the Public Gardens) or the Ritz-Carlton Dining Room in the Ritz-Carlton-Boston. Cost: $35 per person at the Four Seasons and $42 per person at the Ritz.

CONNECTICUT

HONEYMOON NO. 2 — MYSTIC — STONINGTON

Route
- Highway 1 west out of Westerly to Stonington and Mystic.

Romantic Appeal
- Colonial nostalgia, crisp sea air and clipper ships make for an intriguing honeymoon.

Free Attractions
- Self-guided walking tour of Mystic called The Walk of the Town. Tapes and headsets can be rented from the Chamber of Commerce, 2 Roosevelt Avenue.
- Window-shop at The Olde Mystick Village, off Highway 95 at Coogan Boulevard.
- Walk along the harbor in Stonington.

Low-Cost Attractions
- Denison Homestead on Pequotsepos Road. Cost: $2.50.
- Mystic Marinelife Aquarium, exit 90 off Highway 95. Cost: $8.25.
- Mystic Seaport Museum, on Highway 27. Cost: $1.
- Whitehall Mansion, north of exit 90 off Highway 95. Cost: $2.
- Old Lighthouse Museum, 7 Water Street, Stonington. Cost: $2.

Special Splurges
- Voyager Cruises, which leave from Steamboat Wharf in Mystic. Cost: Half-day and sunset cruises — $26 per person; one-day cruises — $55 per person.
- Stay at The Inn at Mystic, overlooking the Mystic River. Ask for a gatehouse room with a fireplace. Enjoy swimming in the pool, soaking in the whirlpool, boating and canoeing in the bay, and fishing and tennis. Cost: Two people/one bed; about $100 per night.
- Take in Sunday brunch at the Flood Tide Restaurant. Cost: About $40 for two.

VERMONT

HONEYMOON NO. 3 — LAKE CHAMPLAIN

Route
- Highway 89 northwest out of Montpelier to Highway 100.
- Highway 100 north of Highway 89 to Stowe.
- Highway 108 north out of Stowe to Jeffersonville.
- Highway 104 west out of Jeffersonville to St. Albans, Swanton and Lake Champlain Island.

Romantic Appeal

- Relax and unwind on the open expanses of Lake Champlain, watch for Champ, the lake's own Loch Ness Monster, and lose yourselves on this water honeymoon.

Free Attractions

- Walking tours of Stowe, St. Albans, Swanton and Jeffersonville.
- Hike along the banks of Lake Champlain.
- Hyde Log Cabin on the main road in Grand Isle.
- St. Anne's Shrine on Isle LaMotte.
- Attend Stowe's Winter Carnival, if you're honeymooning in mid-January, the Stowe Derby in February, or the Sugar Slalom in April.
- Hike along the Stowe Recreation Path that starts in Stowe Center. It is a five-mile scenic pathway that follows the mountain stream toward Mount Mansfield.
- Mary Bryan Art Gallery on Main Street in Jeffersonville.

Low-Cost Attractions

- St. Albans Historical Museum, Church and Bishop streets. Cost: $1.
- Stowe Alpine Slide, 7½ miles north on Highway 108. Cost: $6, or $24 for five rides.
- Stowe Gondola, 7½ miles northwest of Stowe on Highway 108. Cost: Round-trip $9.50.
- Stowe Auto Road, five miles northwest of Stowe off Highway 108. Cost: $10 per car.

Special Splurges

- Butternut Inn at Stowe has eight acres of landscaped grounds, rooms decorated in period antiques, afternoon tea with home-baked chocolate chip cookies, a heated pool by the mountain stream, and a full breakfast included in the price. This inn is called "a true couples' getaway" and they especially cater to honeymooners. Cost: Two people/ one bed, starts at about $95 per night.
- Have dinner at Ten Acres Lodge dining room, at Ten Acres Lodge, 14 Barrows Road in Stowe, where you will have an elegant, candlelit meal. Cost: About $80 for two.

NEW HAMPSHIRE

Honeymoon No. 4 — The White Mountains

Route

- Highway 93 north out of Concord to Franconia.
- Highway 302 east out of Franconia to Crawford, Notch, Franconia Notch, Bartlett and Jackson Glen.
- Highway 16 north out of Jackson Glen to Pinkham Notch.

Romantic Appeal

- When you feel a little tired and chilled after your mountain hike, cuddle up in front of the fireplace in your rustic honeymoon cottage.

Free Attractions

- Swim at Echo Lake, at the north end of Franconia Notch.
- Hike to the Basin, reached by trail from Highway 3 north of the Flume in Franconia Notch, where you will see a waterfall and a deep glacial pothole rimmed by polished stones.
- Hike to Arethusa Falls, 1½ miles from the highway in Crawford Notch.

Low-Cost Attractions

- The Frost Place, at exit 38 off Highway 92 to Highway 116. This is the house poet Robert Frost purchased in 1915. Cost: $3.
- New England Ski Museum, beside the Cannon Mountain Aerial Tramway in Franconia. Cost: $1.
- Cannon Mountain Aerial Tramway II, ½ mile north of the Profile at Franconia Notch. Cost: $7.
- The Flume, located at the southern end of Franconia Notch, is a chasm with 90-foot-high granite walls, waterfalls and a stream. Cost: $5.50.
- Attitash Alpine Slide on Highway 302 in Bartlett. Cost: $8.
- Wildcat Mountain Gondola Tramway, on Highway 16, Pinkham Notch. Cost: $6.50.

Special Splurges

- Mount Washington Cog Railway, northwest of Bretton Woods on Highway 302, then 6 miles northeast on a marked road. A three-hour round-trip to the top of Mount Washington. Cost: $32 per person.
- Rent a cottage with a fireplace at Lovett's Inn By Lafayette Brook in Franconia. There is a heated pool, fishing and cross-country skiing available. Cost: Two people/one bed, starts at about $95 per night.
- Enjoy dinner at this same inn, specializing in regional dishes. Cost: $80 for two.

MAINE

Honeymoon No. 5 — Rockport — Rockland — Camden

Route

- Highway 1 south out of Belfast to Camden, Rockport and Rockland.

Romantic Appeal

- You'll become one with the sea as you jog along the beaches, ferry to nearby islands, or watch the schooner races.

Free Attractions

- Walking tours of Camden, Rockland and Rockport.
- Free entertainment galore in the summer, particularly at Camden's schooner races, art shows, folk festivals, antique shows and lobster festivals. There are also festivals at other times of the year, including the Camden Fall Festival in early October and Christmas by the Sea, a traditional New England celebration.
- Hike through Camden Hills State Park, 2 miles north of Camden on Highway 1, for a scenic view of Camden village and harbor.
- People-watch along the wharf in Rockland.
- Enjoy free entertainment in Rockland throughout the year, including the Schooner Days celebration in July and the Maine Lobster Fest the first weekend in August.
- Shore Village Museum (Maine's lighthouse museum) at 104 Limerock Street, Rockland.
- Vinalhaven Historical Society Museum, on Vinalhaven Island (a ferry ride from Rockland).
- Hike along the trails and rocky beaches of Vinalhaven Island.

Low-Cost Attractions

- Old Conway House and Museum, 1 mile south via Highway 1 in Camden. Cost: $2.
- Farnsworth Art Museum and Homestead, 19 Elm Street, Rockland. Cost: $3.
- Owls Head Transportation Museum, 2 miles south on Highway 73, Rockland. Cost: $4.
- Take a ferry ride from Rockland to Vinalhaven Island. Cost: $20 per car.

Special Splurges

- Stay at Samoset Resort on Highway 1 in Rockland where you can enjoy a room overlooking the ocean, plus two swimming pools, whirlpools, fishing, tennis, rental bicycles, golf, racquetball and a health club. Cost: Two people/one bed, starts at about $100 per night.
- Eat at this same resort in Marcel's. Cost: About $60 for two.

RHODE ISLAND

HONEYMOON NO. 6 — NEWPORT

Route

- Highway 195 southeast out of Providence to Highway 138.
- Highway 138 south to Newport.

Romantic Appeal

- Honeymoon in the "lifestyle of the rich and famous" as you enjoy the beaches, resorts and ponds of Newport.

Free Attractions

- Walk along Newport's famous beaches, including Gooseberry Beach, Sachuest Beach and Hazard's Beach.
- Take the Cliff Walk (it's narrow and dangerous, so wear good hiking shoes) for three miles between Easton Beach and Bailey's Beach.
- Take the walking tour of Newport itself, including Newport's Point and central Newport.
- Window-shop at the Brick Marketplace, America's Cup Avenue and Thames Street.
- Trinity Church, Queen Anne Square.
- Take a drive along Ocean Drive, a 9½ mile circuit offering panoramas of the Atlantic coastline and large summer homes.
- Old Stone Mill, in Touro Park, Bellevue Avenue.

Low-Cost Attractions

- The Astor's Beechwood Mansion, 580 Bellevue Avenue. Cost: $7.
- The Breakers, on Ochre Point Avenue at Ruggles Avenue, is Newport's most splendid mansion. Cost: $7.50.
- Chateau-Sur-Mer on Bellevue Avenue is another mansion. Cost: $6.
- The Elms mansion on Bellevue Avenue. Cost: $6.
- Hammersmith Farm on Ocean Drive. Cost: $6.
- Hunter House, 54 Washington Street. Cost: $6.
- Museum of Yachting in Fort Adams State Park. Cost: $3.
- Newport Art Museum, 76 Bellevue Avenue. Cost: $2.
- Newport Trolley, departs from 23 America's Cup Avenue. Cost: All-day fare $7.50.
- Old Colony and Newport Railroad trips, America's Cup Avenue and Bridge Street. Cost: Round-trip fare: $6.
- Oldport Harbor Tours depart from the Oldport Marina at the Newport Yachting Center on America's Cup Avenue. Cost: One-hour cruise for $6.

Special Splurges

- Stay at the Brinley Victorian Inn, 23 Brinley Street. It is an 1870 bed-and-breakfast with Victorian furnishings. Cost: Two people/one bed, starts at about $85 per night and includes breakfast.
- Enjoy Sunday brunch at The Inn at Castle Hill, 590 Ocean Avenue, overlooking Narragansett Bay. The brunch includes free entertainment, a jazz concert out on the lawn. Cost: $13.50 per person.

CHAPTER 15

THE LAND OF LOVIN' HOSPITALITY
Affordable Honeymoons in the South Central States
Alabama, Arkansas, Kentucky, Louisiana, Mississippi and Tennessee

ALABAMA

HONEYMOON NO. 1 — MOBILE BAY AND DAUPHIN ISLAND

Route
- Highway 163 south out of Mobile to Mobile Bay and Dauphin Island.

Romantic Appeal
- The allure of sun and sand attracts honeymooners; this setting offers a combination of lazy afternoons on the beach and Mardi Gras craziness at night.

Free Attractions
- Walking tour of Mobile (most beautiful during azalea season, from late March to early April).
- Enjoy the city's many festivals, including the Allied Arts Festival, the Mobile Historic Homes Tour, the Mardi Gras, and the Azalea Trail Festival. The Homes Tour and Azalea Trail Festival are usually in conjunction with Mardi Gras, celebrated late March through early April.
- Bienville Square, bounded by Dauphin, St. Joseph, St. Francis and Conception streets in Mobile.
- Carlen House, 54 Carlen Street, Mobile.
- The Fine Arts Museum of the South, Museum Drive, Mobile.
- Fort Conde, 150 South Royal Street, Mobile.
- The Museum of the City of Mobile, 355 Government Street.
- Phoenix Fire Museum, 203 South Claiborne Street, Mobile.
- Bragg-Mitchell Mansion, 1906 Spring Hill Avenue, Mobile.
- Swim at Bienville Beach on Dauphin Island.
- Hike around Dauphin Island.

Low-Cost Attractions
- Oakleigh Mansion, 350 Oakleigh Place. Cost: $4.
- Conde-Charlotte Museum House, 104 Theatre Street, Mobile. Cost: $3.
- The Exploreum, 1906 Spring Hill Avenue, Mobile. Cost: $3.
- Fort Gaines, East Bienville Boulevard, Dauphin Island. Cost: $2.

Special Splurges

- Stay at least one night at the Stouffer Riverview Plaza Hotel, 64 Water Street, Mobile, where you will enjoy the ambience of a four-star hotel, including the sauna, whirlpool and health club. Cost: About $125 per night.
- If you do stay at the Stouffer, be sure to enjoy dinner at their elegant restaurant, Julia's. Cost: About $75 for two.

ARKANSAS

HONEYMOON NO. 2 — HOT SPRINGS — LAKE HAMILTON

Route

- Highway 30 southwest out of Little Rock to Highway 70.
- Highway 70 west to Hot Springs.

Romantic Appeal

- For those couples who love water sports, the beach and hot thermal baths, this is the ideal honeymoon; they will enjoy the natural beauties of Hot Springs National Park, which encircles a city full of fun.

Free Attractions

- Walking tour of Hot Springs.
- Enjoy the free entertainment available during Hot Springs' festivals, including the Oaklawn Horserace Meet, held during February; the Arkansas Derby Day, early April; and the Arkansas Oktoberfest in mid-October.
- Dryden Potter, 341 Whittington Avenue, Hot Springs. Free tours.
- Hot Springs Arts Center, 514 Central Avenue, Hot Springs. Admittance to the center is free; performance costs vary.

Low-Cost Attractions

- Arkansas Alligator Farm, 847 Whittington Avenue, Hot Springs. If you're into alligators, this will be a lot of fun. Cost: $3.
- Josephine Tussaud Wax Museum, 250 Central Avenue, Hot Springs. Cost: $4.50.
- Mid-America Museum, 400 Mid-America Boulevard, Hot Springs. Cost: $3.95.
- Tiny Town, 374 Whittington Avenue, Hot Springs. This is the fascinating handiwork of one family, including quarter-scale animated replicas of settings such as a farm, sawmill, Indian Village, Wild West town and blacksmith shop. Cost: $2.50.
- Belle of Hot Springs, 4911 Central Avenue, Hot Springs, offers daytime and evening cruises. Cost: $6.99 per person.

- Hot Springs Mountain Observation Tower, Hot Springs Mountain Drive, Hot Springs. Cost: $2.75.

Special Splurges
- You may be able to afford to stay several nights at Lake Hamilton Resort, 3501 Albert Pike Road in Hot Springs, where you will have a lot of built-in things to do, including fishing, tennis, waterskiing, jet skiing and boating. Cost: About $80 per night.
- Enjoy dinner at the Hamilton House, 130 Van Lyell Drive, overlooking Lake Hamilton. Cost: About $75 for two.

KENTUCKY
Honeymoon No. 3 — Louisville and the Ohio River

Romantic Appeal
- From cruising down the Ohio River to exciting nightlife, Louisville offers newlyweds a honeymoon full of fun things to do.

Free Attractions
- Walking tour of Louisville.
- Enjoy the festivities if you happen to be in Louisville during Derby Week; the Kentucky Derby is always held on the first Saturday in May.
- Other festivals include the Bluegrass Music Festival, over Labor Day weekend; Kentucky Music Weekend, late July; and the Shakespearean festival held each summer, mid-June through early August, with free performances. The Christmas in the City celebration occurs throughout downtown and includes ice skating, caroling and a Christmas ball.
- Enjoy Riverfront Plaza in downtown Louisville, a great place for people-watching, as well as a vantage point to view the Louisville Falls Fountain, a floating structure propeling water, colored by the play of 102 lights, 375 feet into the air.
- The Filson Club, 1310 South Third Street, Louisville. This is a Kentuckian museum.
- John Conti Coffee Museum, 4023 Bardstown Road.
- Kentucky Art and Craft Center, 609 West Main Street in the historic district of Louisville.

Low-Cost Attractions
- *The Belle of Louisville*, docked at the foot of Fourth Street, is an old-fashioned stern-wheeler that offers sightseeing cruises on the Ohio River. Cost: $7.
- Enjoy the nightlife in Louisville, found in hotel and restaurant lounges. One very popular spot is the Phoenix Hill, 644 Baxter Avenue.
- Enjoy a horse tram ride from Louisville Horse Trams, Inc., which provides a sightseeing tour through downtown Louisville. A good place to hop on one of these rides is at the

Spaghetti Factory restaurant.

- Locust Grove, a restored 1790 Georgian mansion is located on Blankenbaker Lane. Cost: $3.
- Louisville Zoo, 1100 Trevilian Way. Cost: $4.50.
- Museum of History and Science, 727 West Main Street. Cost: $6 (which includes admission to the Imax theatre).
- Rauch Memorial Planetarium at the University of Louisville. Cost: $3.
- J.B. Speed Art Museum, 2035 South Third Street. Cost: Admission is free; parking is $2.

Special Splurges

- Stay at the Holiday Inn-Southeast, 3255 Bardstown Road. There is a Holidome indoor recreation facility with indoor pool, jacuzzi and weight room. It is also walking distance to miniature golf and bowling, and continental breakfast is included with your room. Cost: About $50 per night.
- How about dinner on a cruise ship? *The Star of Louisville* is docked on the Louisville Wharf at River Road, right on the Ohio River, and departs at noon for lunch, 7 P.M. for dinner, and 1 P.M. for Sunday brunch. Cost: $76 per couple for a dinner cruise on a weekend, including dinner and entertainment. Cash bar is extra.

LOUISIANA

HONEYMOON NO. 4 — SHREVEPORT — BOSSIER CITY

Romantic Appeal

- For those newlyweds looking for a "spicey" honeymoon, this is it! Shreveport-Bossier City is known as the Spice of Louisiana because of its variety of festivals, attractions and food.

Free Attractions

- Enjoy over a dozen free festivals that take place during the year, including Holiday in Dixie (10 days in April), the American Rose Festival (late April), the Tournament of Champions (a waterskiing competition held in July), and the Red River Revel (an eight-day open-air festival of arts held in October).
- Walking tours of the two cities.
- Drive along the south shore of Cross Lake to Ford Municipal Park where you can hike or picnic.
- Barnwell Memorial Garden and Art Center, 501 Clyde Fant Parkway, Shreveport.
- Louisiana State Exhibit Museum, 3015 Greenwood Road, Shreveport.

- Meadows Museum of Art, 2911 Centenary Boulevard, Shreveport.
- R.W. Norton Art Gallery, 4747 Creswell Avenue, Shreveport.

Low-Cost Attractions
- Water Town, 7670 West Seventieth Street, Shreveport. Cost: $9.
- Touchstone's Wildlife and Art Museum, 3386 Highway 80, Bossier City. Cost: $1.

Special Splurges
- Stay a night or two at the Residence Inn by Marriott at 1001 Gould Drive, Bossier City. Ask for a room with a fireplace. There are cable movies, a pool, whirlpools and a sports court. Cost: about $80 per night.
- You'll have to try at least one meal at the pricey Monsieur Patou restaurant at 855 Pierremont Road in Shreveport. This is elegant European dining; you will want to do the "dress-up thing." Cost: About $100 for two.

Note: See chapter 27 for a special feature on New Orleans.

MISSISSIPPI
HONEYMOON NO. 5 — NATCHEZ

Route
- Highway 20 west out of Jackson to Vicksburg.
- Highway 61 south out of Vicksburg to Natchez.

Romantic Appeal
- Newlyweds will step back into the nineteenth century in this historical honeymoon setting with its horse-drawn carriages, antebellum mansions and Mississippi riverboat cruises.

Free Attractions
- Walking tour of Natchez.
- Stroll along the banks of the Mississippi River.
- People-watch in the downtown center of Natchez.

Low-Cost Attractions
- Weymouth Hall, 1 Cemetery Road, on a bluff overlooking the Mississippi River. Cost: $4.
- Stanton Hall, 401 High Street, is one of America's largest antebellum mansions. Cost: $2.
- Ravennaside, 601 South Union Street, offers guided tours. Cost: $2.

- Natchez Pilgrimage Tours, Canal and State streets downtown, offers tours of various nineteenth-century antebellum homes. Cost: five-house tour for about $17; three-house tour for about $12.
- Natchez Carriage Company offers horse-drawn carriage tours of downtown Natchez, departing from the Natchez Eola Hotel at 110 North Pearl Street. Cost: $8 per person.
- During the Natchez Pilgrimages, held biannually (March 7 through April 7 and October 6 through 26), there are many events that take place, all with varying admission charges. Some of these events are the Mississippi Medicine Show, concerts by the Voices of Hope Singers, the melodrama "The Drunkard," and the Great Mississippi River Balloon Race, craft fairs, Indian fairs and musical entertainment.

Special Splurges

- Stay at least one night at the Monmouth Plantation, which calls itself "a glorious return to the antebellum South." There are 26 acres of landscaped grounds, exquisite rooms with antique furniture, and a full Southern breakfast is included during your stay. It has been rated as one of the 10 most romantic places in the U.S.A. by *USA Today* and *Glamour* magazine. Cost: About $100 per night.
- If you have any appetite left after their ample breakfasts, you may want to enjoy a five-course dinner at the Monmouth Plantation. Cost: About $100 for two.

TENNESSEE

HONEYMOON NO. 6 — PIGEON FORGE — GATLINBURG — GREAT SMOKY MOUNTAINS

Route

- Highway 441 southeast out of Knoxville to Pigeon Forge, Gatlinburg and Great Smoky Mountains National Park.

Romantic Appeal

- Honeymooners thrive on the fun and entertainment found in this part of Tennessee; when things get too exciting they retreat to nature where the blue, smoke-like haze of the Smoky Mountains offers an umbrella of tranquility.

Free Attractions

- Walking tours of Pigeon Forge and Gatlinburg.
- Shop at the Belz Factory Outlet Mall on the Parkway, off Highway 441.
- Pigeon Forge Pottery on Middle Creek Road offers tours and demonstrations.
- Hike and picnic along the shores of the Little Pigeon River.
- Take the 11-mile loop road tour of Cades Cove in Great Smoky Mountains National

Park, followed by a free tour of the mill area with park rangers as your guides.

- Enjoy Cataloochee, 21 miles north of Waynesville via Highway 276 through Cove Creek Gap. It is a secluded area that has interesting historical buildings and some good trout fishing, if you're in the mood for that kind of thing.

Low-Cost Attractions

- Rainbow Music Theatre, 1100 North Parkway, Pigeon Forge, presents a variety show mix of country, gospel, pop and comedy. Cost: $8.80.
- American Historical Wax Museum, 544 Parkway, Gatlinburg. Cost: $4.
- Christus Gardens, 275 River Road, Gatlinburg, contains dioramas depicting scenes from the life of Christ, costumed figures, and a collection of Biblical coins. Cost: $5.
- Guinness World Records Museum at Baskins Square Mall in Gatlinburg. Cost: $4.95.
- Ober Gatlinburg on Mt. Harrison in Gatlinburg, is a theme park and recreation complex that offers ice skating, winter skiing, an alpine slide, shopping, crafts, cafes and live entertainment. The access road is very dangerous; the best way to get to the park is to take the sightseers chairlift or the aerial tramway. Cost: Chairlift and tramway, about $6 per person per round-trip. Admission to the complex itself is $3 with additional charges for the various activities. For example, three hours of ice skating, including skate rental, is $5 per person.

Special Splurges

- Take in the Dixie Stampede, 1 mile northeast of Pigeon Forge on Highway 441, which offers a program of music, comedy, rodeo and Wild West-style performances, plus a country-style meal. Cost: $23.96 per person.
- Dollywood, 1 mile northeast of Pigeon Forge on Highway 441, is a theme park with rides and attractions, as well as the Dolly Parton Museum. There are more than 25 live musical performances daily. Cost: $19.75 per person.
- You may be able to stay several nights at Deer Ridge Mountain Resort on old Highway 73 in Gatlinburg. Every room has a fireplace and a balcony that overlooks mountain surroundings. This resort is at an isolated mountaintop location and has four swimming pools, a sauna, whirlpool, tennis courts and steamroom. Cost: About $85 per night.
- You must try the Peddler Restaurant at 1113 River Road in Gatlinburg. It sits right on Little Pigeon River and specializes in aged beef and charcoal grilled entrees. Call ahead and ask for a table that overlooks the river. Cost: About $50 for two.

CHAPTER 16

THE LAND OF WIND AND WATER

Affordable Great Lakes Honeymoons

Illinois, Indiana, Michigan, Minnesota, Ohio and Wisconsin

ILLINOIS

HONEYMOON NO. 1 — PEORIA AND THE ILLINOIS RIVER

Romantic Appeal
- Whether taking a gambler's riverboat ride on the Illinois River or walking hand in hand through Wildlife Prairie Park, Peoria is idyllic for honeymooners.

Free Attractions
- Take a glass-enclosed elevator ride to the top of the water tower at Tower Park, Prospect Road at Glen Avenue, where you'll have a superb view of the Illinois River and downtown Peoria.
- Walking tour of Peoria.
- Hike through Forest Park Nature Center, off Prospect Road in Peoria Heights.
- Attend a free concert at the Courthouse Plaza at Main Street and Adams Avenue, May through September.
- Attend one of Peoria's many free festivals, including Steamboat Days, a three-day festival on the waterfront in June, and the Festival of Lights from late November to early January.
- Lakeview Museum of Arts and Sciences, 1125 West Lake Avenue.
- Hang out along the waterfront; people-watch.
- Hike through Fort Crevecoeur Park, two blocks north of Highway 29 in Creve Coeur, overlooking the Illinois River.

Low-Cost Attractions
- Glen Oak Park, McClure and Prospect avenues, has a zoo, conservatory, gardens, floral displays and offers outdoor entertainment during the summer. Cost: $2.
- Lakeview Planetarium at Lakeview Museum of Arts and Sciences. Cost: $2.25.
- Wheels O' Time Museum, 11923 North Knoxville Avenue. Cost: $3.
- Wildlife Prairie Park, 4 miles south off Highway 74 at exit 82, has a visitor center, museum, pioneer farmstead, country store and a narrow gauge railroad, plus 1,850 acres of lakes and forests. Cost: $4.
- Take a two-hour cruise on the *Par-a-dice* steamboat. It departs from the foot of Main street and cruises to Peoria Lake and back. Cost: $7.95 to $10.95.

Special Splurges

- You may be able to afford several nights at the Mark Twain Hotel, 225 Northeast Adams. Ask for a room with a river view and a whirlpool bath. Cost: $65 to $75 per night.
- Have an early bird special at the River Station Restaurant, right on the river at 212 Constitution Avenue. Cost: About $50 for two.

Note: See chapter 27 for a special feature on Chicago.

INDIANA

Honeymoon No. 2 — "Big Cave Country" — Corydon

Route

- Highway 62 west out of New Albany to Corydon.

Romantic Appeal

- Explore the rivers, forests and caves near old Corydon, the historical setting for this dream honeymoon.

Free Attractions

- Walking tour of old Corydon.
- Hike through the Wyandotte Woods State Recreation Area in Harrison-Crawford State Forest, which overlooks the Ohio River.
- Hang out at Old Capital Square. It has lots of shops that sell local art, solid wood furniture, antiques and other specialties.
- Corydon Capitol State Historic Site, downtown Corydon, is an interesting place to explore.
- Zimmerman Art Glass Company, 395 Valley Road, is famous for its paperweights, bottles and bowls. They give glass sculpting demonstrations on Tuesdays through Fridays.

Low-Cost Attractions

- Squire Boone Caverns and Village, exit 105 off Highway 64, provides a whole day's worth of fun. There are cavern tours, hayrides, craft demonstrations, a zoo, an Indian museum, nature trail, and lots of interesting shops. Cost: About $9.50.
- Wyandotte Caves, on Wyandotte Cave Road in nearby Leavenworth, offers a tour of Big Wyandotte Cave, which was used by prehistoric Indians. Be sure to wear a warm jacket and dependable walking shoes. Cost: $3.75.
- Little Wyandotte Cave, at the same location, has a variety of cave formations that can be seen on a guided tour. Cost: $2.75.

Special Splurges

- Kintner House Inn at 101 South Capitol Avenue is a very "honeymoony" historical bed-and-breakfast. The inn is completely restored and each room is filled with antiques. Ask for a room with a fireplace. Cost: About $65 per night.

MICHIGAN

HONEYMOON NO. 3 — MACKINAC ISLAND — MACKINAW CITY

Route

- Highway 75 north out of Flint to Mackinaw City.
- A ferry ride from Mackinaw City to Mackinac Island.

Romantic Appeal

- A sugar sand beach, a carriage ride, and a summer concert on the lawn will create cherished honeymoon memories.

Free Attractions

- Hike around Mackinac Island (Mackinac means "Old Turtle"), which is 3 miles long and 2 miles wide. There are caves, ravines, rocks and arches to explore.
- Early Missionary Bark Chapel, in Marquette Park on Mackinac Island, is a reconstruction of the original chapel built in the late 1600s.
- The Mackinaw Bridge Museum on Central Avenue in downtown Mackinaw City has all kinds of memorabilia and artifacts that pertain to the building of Mackinaw Bridge.
- A walking tour of downtown Mackinaw City.

Low-Cost Attractions

- Take a carriage tour of Mackinac Island's scenic and historical spots. Cost: $11.
- Fort Mackinac on Mackinac Island is on a bluff above the harbor and has several attractions, including the Beaumont Memorial, the Benjamin Blacksmith Shop, the Biddle House, the Indian Dormitory, the McGulpin House, and the Stuart House Museum. Cost: $6.50-$11, plus an additional $1 per person to see the Stuart House Museum.
- Colonial Michilimackinac offers a day's worth of entertainment. There are costumed reenactments, exhibits, blacksmithing and cooking demonstrations, a colonial wedding and the "arrival of the French voyageurs." You can also go on an archaeological excavation. Cost: $6.
- Mill Creek State Historic Park, on Highway 23 out of Mackinaw City, is the site of an eighteenth-century complex with a sawmill, houses, nature trails, scenic overlooks and archaeological digs. Cost: $4.

- Teysen's Woodland Indian Museum, 416 South Huron Avenue, Mackinaw City, displays dioramas and pioneer and Indian artifacts dating back to 9000 B.C. Cost: $2.

Special Splurges
- Spend some time at the Travelodge, 905 South Huron Street, right on Lake Huron. Ask for a honeymoon suite with a lakefront view and private balcony. There is a private sandy beach, an indoor heated pool, a whirlpool and free movies. Cost: About $55 per night.
- Have breakfast at Murray's Restaurant at Mackinac Island's 100-year-old Murray Hotel. Their breakfasts are feasts and you will have a picturesque view. Cost: About $30 for two.

MINNESOTA
Honeymoon No. 4 — Great River Road

Route
- Highway 61 south out of Minneapolis, along the Mississippi River to Hastings, Red Wing, Frontenac, Lake City, Wabasha and Winona.

Romantic Appeal
- Honeymooners linger in these historic river towns along Great River Road, exploring their shops and museums, strolling along their riverfronts, and enjoying the scenic expanse of water and bluffs.

Free Attractions
- Walking tours of the six river towns.
- Hike along the riverfronts of the Mississippi River.
- Enjoy a tour and tasting at the Alexis Bailly Vineyard and Winery in Hastings.
- Walk along the observation platform at Dam No. 2's recreation area in Hastings, where you can watch barges, cruisers and canoes pass through the lock.
- Hike in the summer or snowshoe in the winter through the Carpenter-St. Croix Valley Nature Center along the St. Croix River at 12805 St. Croix Trail in Hastings.
- Enjoy Hasting's free entertainment during the Front Porch Festival, held every May. Also, in late July Hastings celebrates Rivertown Days with hot-air balloons, a boat parade, live music and a fireworks display.
- Red Wing has some fun festivals, too, including Shiver River Days in January and River City Days in August.
- American Museum of Wildlife Art, 3303 North Service Drive, Red Wing.
- Garvin Heights Scenic Wayside on Highway 61 in Winona affords a panoramic view of

the Mississippi River Valley.

- Polish Cultural Institute, 102 Liberty Street in Winona, exhibits a collection of artifacts of local Polish history.

Low-Cost Attractions

- Take a sightseeing cruise on the *Spirit of Lake City* in McHill Park off Highway 61 in Lake City. Cost: $7.95.
- Arrowhead Bluffs Museum on Highway 60 in Wabasha has a large collection of Native American and pioneer artifacts. Cost: $3.25.
- Bunnell House on Highway 14/61 in Homer, near Winona, was the home of an early settler. Cost: $2.

Special Splurges

- Stay at least one night at the St. James Hotel in Red Wing. It is a restored 1875 Victorian hotel that lends itself to honeymoon romance. Cost: About $100 per night.
- The Port of Red Wing Restaurant is in this same hotel and is perfect for an elegant dinner. Cost: About $75 for two.

OHIO

HONEYMOON NO. 5 — KELLEYS ISLAND — SANDUSKY

Route

- Highway 2 east out of Toledo to Sandusky.
- Ferryboat from Sandusky to Kelleys Island.

Romantic Appeal

- Combine the privacy and seclusion of Kelleys Island with the thrills of Cedar Point Theme Park and you have an awarding-winning honeymoon.

Free Attractions

- Hike around Kelleys Island State Park; see the Glacial Grooves.
- Walking tour of Sandusky.
- Shop at the Lake Erie Factory Outlet Center in Sandusky.
- Take a tour through the Firelands Winery at 917 Bardshar Road in Sandusky, and then eat a bring-your-own lunch in their enchanting picnic area.
- Walk along Sandusky Bay.
- Follett House Museum at 404 Wayne Street in Sandusky is an 1827 mansion furnished with intriguing old toys and household items.

Low-Cost Attractions

- Merry-Go-Round Museum, at the corner of West Washington and Jackson streets in Sandusky. Cost: $2.50.

Special Splurges

- Spend two entire days at Cedar Point off Highway 6, 10 miles north of the Ohio Turnpike at exit 7. It is a 364-acre amusement/theme park and resort. There are rides, theatres, midways, live musical reviews, Jungle Larry's Safari, performing dolphins and sea lions, waterslides and a beach. Cost: About $22 per person per day.
- Stay at least one night at the Radisson Harbour Inn at the Cedar Point Causeway in Sandusky. It is right on the water and has an indoor heated pool, whirlpool and free movies. You can even fish off their dock. Cost: About $100 per night and up.

WISCONSIN

HONEYMOON NO. 6—WISCONSIN DELLS

Route

- Highway 51 north out of Madison to Highway 16.
- Highway 16 east off Highway 51 to Wisconsin Dells.

Romantic Appeal

- Whether you're snowmobiling in the winter or river cruising in the summer, the Wisconsin Dells offer unsurpassed scenery for the enjoyment of honeymooners.

Free Attractions

- Walking tour of Wisconsin Dells.
- Cross-country skiing in Devil's Lake State Park and Mirror Lake State Park.
- Enjoy Wisconsin Dells' festivals. These include the Wisconsin Dells Balloon Rally in May, the Annual Polish Fest in September, the Annual Heritage Day Celebration in June, the Winery Harvest Fest in October, the Steam Train Autumn Color Tours in October, the Wisconsin Dells Polka Fest in November, the Wisconsin Dells Flake Out Festival in February, and the Wisconsin Sled Dog Championships in February.

Low-Cost Attractions

- Dells Boat Tours at 11 Broadway offers sightseeing trips through the Upper and Lower dells of the Wisconsin River. Cost: A two-and-a-half-hour tour—$9.95; a one-hour tour—$6.50.
- Dells Auto Museum at 591 Wisconsin Dells Parkway. Cost: $3.50.
- Chapel Museum/Norman Rockwell Art on Highway 12. Cost: $2.
- Lost Canyon horse-drawn wagon rides (on Canyon Road). Cost: $5.

- Noah's Ark water park on Highway 23. Cost: $15.95.
- Ripley's Believe It or Not! Museum at 115 Broadway. Cost: $4.50.
- Riverview Park and Waterworld on Highway 12. Cost: $7.95.
- Tommy Bartlett's Ski, Sky and Stage Show at 560 Wisconsin Dells Parkway features a Laser-Rama Light Show, variety acts, and water-skiing show. Cost: $8.95.
- Wax World of the Stars at 105 Broadway displays more than 100 life-like figures. Cost: $4.50.
- Wisconsin Deer Park on Highway 12 is a 28-acre wildlife park. Cost: $4.50.
- Wisconsin Ducks, Inc., on Highway 12, offers one-hour land and water tours along the Wisconsin River. Cost: $9.95.
- Wisconsin Opry on Highway 12 presents country music by local and national professional performers. Cost: $8.50.

Special Splurges

- Try to stay at least one night at the Mayflower II Celebration Suites at 930 Wisconsin Dells Parkway in Wisconsin Dells. Ask for a room with a canopied king-size waterbed and private jacuzzi. Enjoy their suntan bed and electric massage table, plus their two swimming pools and game room. Cost: About $125 per night.
- Enjoy dinner at Ishnaia Restaurant in Lake Delton where you will have a panoramic view of Mirror Lake plus entertainment. Cost: About $60 for two.

CHAPTER 17

The Land of Sand, Surf and Seashells
Affordable Southeastern Honeymoons
Florida, Georgia, North Carolina and South Carolina

FLORIDA

Honeymoon No. 1 — Bradenton — Sarasota

Route
- Highway 75 south out of Tampa to Bradenton-Sarasota.

Romantic Appeal
- Honeymooners have miles of white, sandy beaches to choose from on Sarasota Bay and the clear Gulf waters are ideal for body surfing. Add to this the dozens of things to do and see, and your days will be delightfully balanced between soaking up the sun and "go-see-do."

Free Attractions
- Walking tours of Sarasota and Bradenton.
- Enjoy a free water show in Island Park, Sarasota, presented every Sunday from late January through March.
- The Royal Lipizzan Stallions can be seen, also from January through March, as they are trained at Colonel Herrman's Ranch in Manatee county on Singletary Road.
- Manatee Village Historical Park, Sixth Avenue East and Fifteenth Street East.

Low-Cost Attractions
- Bellm Cars and Music of Yesterday, one block south of the airport in Sarasota. Cost: $6.50.
- Marie Selby Botanical Gardens, 811 South Palm Avenue, Sarasota. Cost: $5.
- Mote Marine Science Aquarium, the south end of New Pass Bridge, Sarasota. Cost: $5.
- Myakka Wildlife Tours, 9 miles east of Highway 75 at exit 37 offers narrated tram tours in Myakka River State Park. Cost: $6.
- The Ringling Museum of Art, west of Highway 41 at the Sarasota/Bradenton Airport. Cost: $8.50.
- Sarasota Jungle Gardens, 3701 Bayshore Road. Cost: $7.
- South Florida Museum and Bishop Planetarium, 201 Tenth Street West. Cost: $5.

Special Splurges

- Stay at least one night at the Hyatt Sarasota, 1000 Boulevard of the Arts in Sarasota. It overlooks Sarasota Bay and offers lots of amenities, including a marina with sailing and cruising boats available. Cost: Two people/one bed, starts at about $115 per night.

GEORGIA

HONEYMOON NO. 2 — "THE GOLDEN ISLANDS" — JEKYLL, CUMBERLAND, SEA ISLAND AND ST. SIMONS

Route

- Highway 95 south out of Savannah to Brunswick.
- Highway 50 east out of Brunswick to Jekyll Island.
- Toll bridge from Brunswick to Sea Island.

Romantic Appeal

- Honeymooners thrive on white sand beaches, sea breezes and salty air, an idyllic setting in which to relax and enjoy newly married life.

Free Attractions

- Play in the sand dunes at Cumberland Island National Seashore.
- Swim and hike along the 10-mile beach on Jekyll Island.
- Arthur Moore Methodist Museum at Epworth-by-the-Sea on St. Simons Island.
- Christ Church, south of Fort Frederica National Monument.
- Fort Frederica National Monument, St. Simons Island, offers a self-guided tour and an historical film.
- Walking tour of Brunswick.

Low-Cost Attractions

- Take a ferry ride to Cumberland Island. Cost: $7.95.
- Take a ferry ride to Plum Orchard mansion any Sunday from April through September, or the first Sunday of each month during the rest of the year. Cost: $6.
- Jekyll Island Club Historic District tour, including a ride aboard an open-air tram. Cost: $7.
- Summer Waves, 210 South Riverview Drive, Jekyll Island, is an 11-acre water park. Cost: $9.95.
- Museum of Coastal History, 101 Twelfth Street, St. Simons Island, a lighthouse keeper's restored home.
- Hofwyl-Broadfield Plantation, 10 miles north on Highway 17 in Brunswick. Cost: $1.50.

Special Splurges

- You may be able to afford several nights at the Radisson Resort Hotel, Jekyll Island Club, 371 Riverview Drive. Located on the beach, this hotel also offers a heated pool, rental bicycles, whirlpool baths, golf and tennis. Cost: Two people/one bed, starts at about $69 per night.
- You have to try Blackbeards Restaurant, 200 North Beachview Drive, Jekyll Island. Go when you're hungry because the portions are huge. You'll have an ocean view. Cost: About $50 for two.

NORTH CAROLINA

Honeymoon No. 3 — "The Outer Banks"

Route

- Highway 70 east out of Raleigh to Atlantic City and Beaufort.
- Highway 12 north out of Beaufort to the Outer Banks Islands.

Romantic Appeal

- Unspoiled, primitive and wild, these islands are enjoyed by nature lovers and are perfect for honeymooners who want to get out of the fast lane and just enjoy each other for a while.

Free Attractions

- Fort Macon State Park, 2 miles east of Highway 1190 at Atlantic Beach. Fort Macon includes a museum.
- North Carolina Aquarium at Pine Knoll Shores, 5 miles west of Atlantic Beach on Highway 58N.
- The Lindsay Warren Visitor Center at Fort Raleigh National Historic Site on Roanoke Island, 3 miles north of Manteo.
- Jockey's Ridge State Park, off the Highway 158 bypass at Nags Head on the Outer Banks.
- North Carolina Maritime Museum, 315 Front Street, Beaufort.
- Walking tours of Bath, Beaufort, Hatteras, Nags Head and Manteo.

Low-Cost Attractions

- Elizabethan Gardens at Fort Raleigh National Historic Site. Cost: $2.50.
- Wright Brothers National Monument on the outer banks, Highway 158 bypass at Milepost 8 in Kill Devil Hills, has a visitor exhibit that includes a full-scale reproduction of the 1902 and 1903 gliders. Cost: $1.
- "The Lost Colony" presented in the Waterside Theater, 3 miles northwest of Manteo on Roanoke Island, is an outdoor symphonic drama. Cost: $10.

- Elizabeth II State Historic Park, across from Manteo's waterfront at Manteo on Roanoke Island. Cost: $3.
- Historic Bath Site, on Highway 92. Bath, the oldest town in North Carolina, offers tours of restored houses from its visitor center. A film precedes the tour. Cost: About $2 per person.
- Mystery Tours, depart from Beaufort Waterfront in Beaufort. Cost: $8.
- Old Town Beaufort Historic Site tour, begins at 138 Turner Street (the Josiah Bell House). Cost: $5.

Special Splurges

- The Nags Head Inn at Nags Head is a great place to honeymoon, and you may be able to afford several nights because their rates are reasonable. All their rooms are ocean-front with balconies. They have a heated pool whirlpool, fishing and golf. Cost: Two people/one bed, ranges from $45 to $105 per night starting rate, depending on the time of the year.
- Have lunch at the Beaufort House, on the boardwalk in Beaufort. They have a large second-story deck that overlooks the entire marina. Cost: About $5 for two.

SOUTH CAROLINA

HONEYMOON NO. 4 — HILTON HEAD ISLAND

Route

- Highway 26 southeast out of Columbia to Highway 95.
- Highway 95 south off Highway 26 to Highway 278.
- Highway 278 east off Highway 95 to Hilton Head Island.

Romantic Appeal

- Mingle with the rich and famous as you hang out at five-star resorts, enjoying the "freebies" along the way — a real glamour honeymoon.

Free Attractions

- Hike and explore in Pinckay National Wildlife Refuge, over the bridge from Hilton Head on Highway 278.
- One of the most popular free attractions on Hilton Head Island is window-shopping; there is an abundance of shops and outdoor markets. Two of the most popular locations are Shelter Cove and Harbor Town.
- Shelter Cove also offers free entertainment on Tuesday evenings during the summer, including a fireworks display.

Low-Cost Attractions

- Enjoy a hike through the Sea Pines Forest Preserve located in the Sea Pine Plantation, Hilton Head Island. Cost: $3 per car.
- The Fun Factory on Arrow Road in Hilton Head offers all kinds of rides, games and miniature golf. Cost: No admission fee; there is a charge for each individual activity.
- Rent fishing poles, bikes, canoes, paddle boats or in-line skates at any number of places around the island. Cost: Typical rental prices, as quoted by Fish Creek Landing at 77 Queens Follie Road are fishing poles—$4 per hour or $10 per day; canoes—$12 per hour for two people; paddle boats—$14 per hour for two people; in-line skates—$4 per hour or $10 for four hours; bicycles—$4 per hour or $10 per day.
- There are several cruise companies that sail out of the marinas on Hilton Head Island. Adventure Cruises, located at Shelter Cove Harbor, offers various cruises including a Dolphin Encounter cruise. Cost: The Dolphin Encounter cruise is $12, and a dinner cruise is $28.
- Go for a horseback ride along the beach. Lawton Stables, at Sea Pines Plantation on Hilton Head Island, rents horses for $20 per hour or $25 for an hour and a half.
- If you happen to be honeymooning at Hilton Head during April or September, you may want to become spectators at one of the professional golf tournaments. Cost: Varies according to the day of the week. Practice rounds are your best buy.

Special Splurges

- The Mariner's Inn, 23 Ocean Drive, Hilton Head Island, has a lot to offer for the money including oceanfront rooms, two swimming pools, saunas, whirlpools, canoes, surf fishing, rental bicycles, sailboats, golf and tennis. Cost: Two people/one bed, starts at about $75.
- Get all dressed up and have dinner at The Barony Grill in The Westin Resort-Port Royal Plantation. Cost: About $80 for two.

CHAPTER 18

THE LAND OF THE GENTEEL SPIRIT
Affordable Honeymoons in the Mid-Atlantic States
Maryland, Delaware, Virginia and West Virginia

MARYLAND

HONEYMOON No. 1 — OCEAN CITY — ASSATEAGUE ISLAND NATIONAL SEASHORE

Route
- Highway 50 east out of Salisbury to Ocean City.
- Highway 50 west from Ocean City to Highway 611.
- Highway 611 to Assateague Island National Seashore.

Romantic Appeal
- Ocean City offers a nice, safe harbor for honeymoon play, whether you're jet skiing, swimming, parasailing, sailboating, or taking a moonlight dinner cruise.

Free Attractions
- Enjoy walking and people-watching along the 10-mile beach and 3-mile boardwalk at Ocean City.
- Hike along the nature trails in Assateague Island National Seashore where you will see free-roaming Chincoteague ponies at play.
- Stop for a visit at the visitor center operated by the National Park Service on Assateague Island. It is located at the bridge approach to the north end of the island.
- Take a walking tour of Ocean City.
- Enjoy Ocean City's annual events, including the Seaside Boat Show in February, the Ward Wildfowl Carving Championship in April, the Spring Fest in May, the White Marlin Festival in August, the Labor Day Festival, the Sunfest in September, and the Bavarian Fest in October.

Low-Cost Attractions
- Frontier Town on Highway 611, Ocean City, depicts the era of the Wild West. Cost: $7.
- Ocean City Wax Museum on the boardwalk at Wicomico Street in Ocean City. Cost: $4.95.
- Boat rentals, equipment for windsurfing, jet skiing, plus parasailing and sailboating are available at several marinas in Ocean City. Cost: The per-hour rate varies, but rental equipment is all reasonably priced.

- Two full-scale amusement parks are available. Cost: Ticket prices vary according to the ride.

Special Splurges
- Try to stay one or two nights at the Princess Royale Ocean Suite Hotel. It offers two swimming pools, beach, sauna, whirlpools and exercise room. Ask about their honeymoon suites. Cost: About $90 per night.
- Enjoy a meal at Fager's Island Restaurant in The Coconut Malorie Hotel where you will have bay front dining. Cost: About $60 for two.

DELAWARE

HONEYMOON NO. 2 — GEORGETOWN — LEWES — REHOBOTH BEACH — DEWEY BEACH

Route
- Highway 13/113 south out of Wilmington to Georgetown.
- Highway 9 east of Georgetown to Lewes.
- Highway 9 west of Lewes to Highway 1.
- Highway 1 south off Highway 9 to Rehoboth Beach and Dewey Beach.

Romantic Appeal
- Honeymooners cuddle as they sail into Lewes' harbor on a sunset cruise; they laugh as they build sand castles on Rehoboth Beach; and they dream as they watch the sunrise from their private deck overlooking a secluded cove.

Free Attractions
- Walking tours of Georgetown and Lewes.
- Hiking along the beaches.
- Enjoy Lewes' festivals, including the Kite Festival on Good Friday, the Zwaanendael Heritage Garden Tour in June, and the Lewes' Open Homes Tour in December.
- Fisher-Martin House in Lewes, a restored eighteenth-century structure, presents changing exhibits.
- Zwaanendael Museum on Savannah Road in Lewes.
- Prime Hook National Wildlife Refuge on Broadkill Beach Road in Lewes offers hiking, canoeing and fishing.
- Enjoy the Sand Castle Building Contest every August on Rehoboth Beach.

Low-Cost Attractions
- Treasures of the Sea, on the campus of Delaware Community College on Highway 18 in Georgetown, displays the jewels, gold and silver coins and bars discovered by trea-

sure-hunter Mel Fisher. Cost: $2.

- Lewes Historic Complex at Shipcarpenter and Third streets in Lewes. Cost: $5.

Special Splurges

- You may be able to afford several nights at the Bay Resort on the bay at Bellevue Street on Dewey Beach, where you can swim, go fishing, crabbing, sailing and windsurfing. Continental breakfast is included. Cost: About $70 per night.
- Chez La Mer Restaurant at 210 Second Street on Rehoboth Beach specializes in local seafood. Cost: About $70 for two.

VIRGINIA

HONEYMOON NO. 3 — VIRGINIA BEACH — NORFOLK

Route

- Highway 44 east out of Norfolk to Virginia Beach.

Romantic Appeal

- Combine beach and boardwalk with a folk festival and fun park and you have a perfect oceanside honeymoon.

Free Attractions

- Walking tours of Virginia Beach and Norfolk.
- Francis Land House, 3131 Virginia Beach Boulevard, Virginia Beach offers tours hosted by guides in period dress.
- General Douglas MacArthur Memorial on City Hall Avenue in Norfolk.
- Hampton Roads Naval Museum on the Norfolk Naval Base at Farragut Avenue and Dillingham Boulevard in Norfolk.

Low-Cost Attractions

- Ocean Breeze Fun Park on General Booth Boulevard, Virginia Beach. Cost: About $15 per person, plus various prices for individual games.
- Adam Thoroughgood House at the junction of highways 13 and 60 in Virginia Beach is a restored seventeenth-century residence. Cost: $2.
- Old Cape Henry Lighthouse at Fort Story in Virginia Beach. Cost: $2.
- Virginia Marine Science Museum on General Booth Boulevard, Virginia Beach. Cost: $4.25.
- Chrysler Museum on Virginia Beach Boulevard in Norfolk. Suggested donation: $2.
- *Harbor Tours*, a replica of a double-decked nineteenth-century Mississippi riverboat, offers narrated cruises that depart from the Waterside at 333 Waterside Drive in Norfolk. Cost: $13.

- Hunter House Victorian Museum, 240 West Freemason Street, Norfolk. Cost: $3.
- Norfolk Botanical Garden, next to the airport in Norfolk. Cost: $2.
- Virginia Zoological Park, 3500 Granby Street in Norfolk. Cost: $2.
- Willoughby-Baylor House, 601 East Freemason Street in Norfolk, is a furnished eighteenth-century townhouse. Cost: $2.

Special Splurges
- Stay at least one night at the Virginia Beach Resort Hotel at 2800 Shore Drive in Virginia Beach. It offers private balconies that overlook an uncrowded beach on Chesapeake Bay, plus tennis, bicycling, free movies, heated indoor and outdoor pools, sauna, whirlpool and health club, all included in the room rate. Cost: About $140 per night. There is a fee for some activities, including golf, sailing, jet skiing and windsurfing.
- Enjoy seafood grilled over mesquite at Orion's Restaurant, located in the Cavalier Hotel at Oceanfront and Forty-second Avenue in Virginia Beach. Cost: About $75 for two.

WEST VIRGINIA

HONEYMOON NO. 4 — CHARLESTON — HUNTINGTON

Route
- Start in Charleston and take the *West Virginia Belle* cruise to Huntington.
- Return to Charleston via bus, arranged by the cruise company.

Romantic Appeal
- From the genteel aura of old Charleston to the mesmerizing beauty of the Ohio River and the hilarity of Camden Park, honeymooners will be caught up in this unreal world of pleasure.

Free Attractions
- Walking tours of Charleston and Huntington.
- Enjoy Charleston's festivals, including the State Jazz Festival in March, the Sternwheel Regatta Festival late August into September, and Vandalia Gathering on Memorial Day weekend.
- The Cultural Center in the Capitol Complex in Charleston has a museum with Civil War and John Brown exhibits, plus a re-creation of a settler's cabin and a country store.

Low-Cost Attractions
- Sunrise Museums, 746 Myrtle Road in Charleston, are housed in two historic mansions on 16 acres. Cost: $2.
- *West Virginia Belle*, departing from 18 Riverwalk Mall on MacCorkle Avenue in Charleston, offers 12-hour cruises to Huntington on the Ohio and Kanawha rivers. Also available

are shorter brunch, sightseeing and dinner cruises. Cost: The full-day Huntington trip, well worth the money, is $76.95 per person. The return bus trip is $12 per person.

- Camden Park, an amusement park just west of Huntington on Highway 60, offers 26 rides, sternwheeler trips, and shows by nationally known recording artists. Cost: $9 per day for unlimited rides.

Special Splurges

- Stay at least one night at the Charleston Marriott Town Center Hotel at 200 Lee Street East in Charleston. It offers free movies, a heated pool, saunas, a whirlpool, tennis, tanning bed and a health club. Their weekend rates are the best. Cost: About $90 to $125 per night.
- In this same hotel you will find the Tarragon Restaurant, which offers elegant dining. You can do the "dress-up thing" for this spot. Cost: About $75 for two.

CHAPTER 19

THE LAND OF GOOD, OLD-FASHIONED FUN

Affordable Honeymoons in the Great Plains States

Iowa, Kansas, Missouri, Nebraska, North Dakota, South Dakota and Oklahoma

IOWA

HONEYMOON NO. 1 — THE QUAD CITIES (BETTENDORF, IOWA; DAVENPORT, IOWA; MOLINE, ILLINOIS; AND ROCK ISLAND, ILLINOIS)

Romantic Appeal

- The Mississippi River is the setting for all this honeymooning fun; it's a good time with cherished memories to be captured on film and videotape.

Free Attractions

- Walking tours of the quad cities.
- Enjoy Davenport's festivals, including the Bix Memorial Jazz Festival in July, the Civil War Muster in September, and the Christmas Walk in December.
- Window-shop along Riverside Mall, Main and Second streets in Davenport, where antiques, collectibles, arts and crafts are featured.
- Davenport Museum of Art, 1737 West Twelfth Street, Davenport.
- Deere & Company, a tractor factory 7 miles south of Moline, Illinois, on John Deere Road, offers free tours.
- Black Hawk State Historic Site on Highway 5 in Rock Island, Illinois, displays Indian relics. It also has a nice park for picnicking, fishing or hiking.
- Mississippi River Visitor Center on Rodman Avenue on Arsenal Island, Rock Island, overlooks Lock and Dam 15 on the Mississippi.
- Rock Island Museum, on Arsenal Island, Rock Island.

Low-Cost Attractions

- Capitol Celebrity Theatre, in the KAHL Building at 330 West Third Street in Davenport, presents nationally known music personalities, with emphasis on country-and-western, folk, and rock 'n' roll performers. Cost: $14.50 per person.
- Niabi Zoo on Highway 6 in Moline, Illinois. Cost: $2.50.
- Schadler's River Adventures, 2501 River Drive, offers narrated sightseeing cruises on the Mississippi River. Cost: $7 per person.
- The Col. Davenport House at Rock Island Arsenal. Cost: $2.

Special Splurges

- *Steamboat Casino River Cruises*, departing from Bettendorf at Highway 61 and Chestnut Street, offers four hours aboard ship with entertainment, meals and gambling. The ship actually cruises the Mississippi from April through October, but stays dockside the rest of the year. Cost: Varies according to type of cruise, time of year and type of meal. $9.95 to $32.95 per person.
- The *President Riverboat Casino*, departing from River Drive at Brady Street in Davenport. This sidewheeler offers four hours aboard ship with entertainment, meals and gambling. Like the *Steamboat Casino River Cruises*, it also stays dockside during the winter. Cost: Ranges from $12 to $27.95.
- You may be able to afford several nights at the four-star Jumer's Castle Lodge at 900 Spruce Hills Drive, Bettendorf. It has two heated pools, saunas, whirlpool, putting green and an exercise room. Cost: About $81 per night.
- Enjoy Sunday brunch at the Rusty Pelican at 125 South Perry Street in Davenport. It is right on the Mississippi River and also has early bird specials. Cost for Sunday brunch: $8.95 per person.

KANSAS

HONEYMOON NO. 2 — KANSAS CITY, KANSAS — KANSAS CITY, MISSOURI

Romantic Appeal

- Whether you're moonlight cruising the Missouri River on the *Missouri River Queen* or enjoying the nightscene with its hot jazz, this honeymoon locale offers up lots of exciting entertainment.

Free Attractions

- Grinter Place State Historic Site, 1420 South Seventy-eighth Street in Kansas City, Kansas, has a two-story 1857 farmhouse with original and period furnishings.
- Hallmark Visitors Center in the Crown Center Complex, Kansas City, Missouri, offers 12 major exhibits.
- The Kemper Gallery at the Kansas City Art Institute, Forty-fourth Street and Warwick Boulevard, Kansas City, Missouri.
- You must see Country Club Plaza, the first totally planned shopping center in the United States. It is huge, covering 55 acres, and includes restaurants and even nightclubs. It is located at Forty-seventh Street and J.C. Nichols Parkway in Kansas City, Missouri. On Thanksgiving evening spectators clamor for the best vantage point to witness its annual Christmas lighting ceremony.

- Another "must-see" is Crown Center, just south of downtown Kansas City, Missouri. This 85-acre futuristic entertainment and retail complex is called a "city within a city." The Center plays host to weekly free concerts featuring well-known artists.
- Kansas City, Missouri's calendar is loaded with events, including one of the three largest St. Patrick's Day parades in the nation, the Kansas City Jazz Festival in August, and the Kansas City Rodeo during the last week of June and the first week of July.
- Enjoy an afternoon at Swope Park, southeast of downtown Kansas City, Missouri, where you can picnic, hike, play golf, go fishing or boating in the summer, or ice skating in the winter. Also, in the summer musicals and popular entertainers are presented nightly in the outdoor Starlight Theatre.

Low-Cost Attractions
- River City, U.S.A., 1 River City Drive in Kansas City, Kansas, offers year-round cruises on the Missouri River aboard the *Missouri River Queen*. You can go on a sightseeing, dinner, moonlight, Sunday brunch, Monday blues or gospel entertainment cruise. Cost: Starts at $5.75 per person.
- John Wornall House, 61st Terrace and Wornall Road in Kansas City, Missouri, is a restored 1858 Greek Revival plantation house with a formal herb garden. Cost: $2.50.
- Kansas City Museum, 3218 Gladstone Boulevard in Kansas City, Missouri. Cost: $3.50.
- Liberty Memorial, overlooking Union Station at Twenty-fifth and Main streets, Kansas City, Missouri. Cost: $1.
- The Nelson-Atkins Museum of Art, Forty-fifth and Oak streets in Kansas City, Missouri. Cost: $4.
- Oceans of Fun, at Parvin Road, exit 54 off Highway 435 in Kansas City, Missouri. Cost: $13.95.
- Kansas City Zoo at Swope Park, southeast of downtown Kansas City, Missouri. Cost: $3.
- Thomas Hart Benton Home and Studio State Historic Site, 3616 Belleview Avenue, Kansas City, Missouri. Cost: $1.25.
- Worlds of Fun, Parvin Road, exit 54 off Highway 435 in Kansas City, Missouri, is a 170-acre theme park with rides, shows, attractions, musical reviews, dolphin show, three roller coasters, and a triple-decker showboat. Cost: $18.95 per person.
- Enjoy horseback riding on the Santa Fe Trail, which begins at Benjamin Ranch, 6401 East Eighty-seventh Street at Highway 435, Kansas City, Missouri. Cost: $15 for the first hour, and $10 for each additional hour.
- Kansas City's night scene, once known as "Little New York," is flourishing. There are clubs and lounges featuring combos, jam sessions, bluegrass, country, rock and folk music. Enjoy the restaurants, lounges and clubs stretching from downtown to Country

Club Plaza. If you like jazz and blues, try Nightmoves at 5110 Northeast Vivion Road. Call (816)931-2888 for a weekly update of jazz offerings around town. Also, pick up a copy of the weekly entertainment newspaper called *The Pitch*, which is available for free at most restaurants and bookstores.

Special Splurges
- The Hyatt Regency Crown Center, 2345 McGee in Kansas City, Missouri, has two heated pools, saunas, whirlpool, tennis and a health club. They also offer entertainment in their lounge. Cost: About $85 per night.
- You have to try a steak at Benton's Steak and Chop House in Westin Crown Center Hotel. If you're a chocoholic, you won't believe their chocolate dessert bar. Cost: About $80 for two.

MISSOURI

HONEYMOON NO. 3 — ST. LOUIS

Romantic Appeal
- St. Louis is an exciting honeymoon locale; it offers a "big city" feel with its upscale shopping, restaurants, hotels and entertainment. Newlyweds thrive on the sensuous food, great festivals and Huck Finn cruises on the Mississippi.

Free Attractions
- Forest Park, bounded by Lindell, Skinker and Kingshighway boulevards, is a great spot to picnic, hike or go for a bike ride. There is also a golf course and skating rink.
- St. Louis Art Museum on Art Hill at Forest Park.
- The Forum, 555 Washington Avenue, is an arts center with exhibits.
- Grant's Farm on Grasvois Road at Grand Road includes a cabin built in 1856 by Ulysses S. Grant. There are 281 acres with a Clydesdale stable, miniature zoo, carriage collection, animal feeding area, deer park, etc., all operated by Anheuser-Busch Company. Free trackless train tours are available.
- Jefferson Barracks Historical Park at Grant Road and Kingston has a number of buildings, including a museum and stable. Bring a picnic. There is a wonderful overlook that provides a view of the Mississippi River.
- Washington University Gallery of Art in Steinberg Hall at Forsyth and Skinker.
- Anheuser-Busch Brewery, Lynch and Thirteenth streets, offers tours of the Clydesdale stables, packaging plant, etc.
- Take a walking tour of St. Louis's historical district by following the Gateway Trail, a self-guided tour that begins at Gateway Arch.
- St. Louis has many annual festivals, including Tourism Week in May, Fourth of July

celebrations that feature fireworks, jet fighters, sky diving and hot-air balloons. In late August and early September there are several events including the Japanese Festival, the Gentry Fair, and the Forest Park Balloon Rally. In late September Bevo Day offers a musical entertainment, arts and crafts, folk dancing and food and drink, along with the Faust Park Folk Festival.

Low-Cost Attractions

- St. Louis Science Center, 5050 Oakland Avenue. Cost: Free admission to the Science Center; $4.75 admission to the Omnimax Theater.
- Campbell House, Fifteenth and Locust streets, is a museum of early St. Louis. Cost: $3.
- Chatillon-DeMenil House, 3352 DeMenil Place. Cost: $2.50.
- Cupples House and McNamee Art Gallery, 3673 West Pine Boulevard (on the St. Louis University campus), was built in 1890 at a cost of $500,000. It is an ornate 42-room Romanesque mansion furnished with antiques. It also includes an art gallery with changing exhibits. Cost: $2.
- Eugene Field House and Toy Museum, 634 South Broadway, is the 1845 home of author Eugene Field. Cost: $2.
- The Gateway Arch plus visitor center and museum. A tram carries visitors to an observation deck at the top of the arch. You can only purchase tram tickets on the day of your ride. Cost: $1; tram cost: $2.50.
- Missouri Botanical Garden, 4344 Shaw Boulevard. Cost: $2.
- St. Louis Sports Hall of Fame, 100 Stadium Plaza (on the Walnut Street side of Busch Stadium). Cost: $2.50.
- Sappington House Complex, 1015 South Sappington Road, displays an 1808 brick home, plus a library and tea room. Cost: $1.
- Take a boat tour of the Mississippi River aboard a nineteenth-century steamboat. The boats, named the *Huck Finn*, *Tom Sawyer* and *Becky Thatcher*, depart from the base of the Gateway Arch and offer one-hour narrated trips. Cost: $7.
- Enjoy St. Louis's nightlife. Look for a copy of the *Riverfront Times*, a weekly publication that offers a calendar of events and available entertainment.

Special Splurges

- Try to afford at least one night at the Hyatt Regency St. Louis Union Station at Eighteenth and Market streets. It is located in an 100-year-old restored Landmark train station that also features over 120 shops and a two-acre lake, all in an enclosed mall. Cost: About $125 per night.
- In this same hotel you will find the Station Grille, a four-star restaurant that features beef and fresh seafood. Cost: About $75 for two.

HONEYMOON NO. 4 — OMAHA — MISSOURI RIVER

Romantic Appeal

- Newlyweds live it up in Nebraska's biggest city; there's everything from water slides, to horse racing, to light shows — pretty big excitement for this small state.

Free Attractions

- Take a walking tour of a historical section of Omaha called Old Market Area, bounded by Tenth, Thirteenth, Howard and Harney streets. This area contains art galleries, boutiques, specialty shops, pubs, restaurants and theaters. A trackless trolley car called *Ollie the Trolley* runs around the area and is a lot of fun, too!
- Just east of this Old Market Area is the Heartland of America Fountain and Park that lies on 110 acres of riverfront and features a 45-minute light show.
- Union Pacific Museum, 1416 Dodge Street, contains furnishings from Abraham Lincoln's funeral railroad card.

Low-Cost Attractions

- Fun Plex Amusement Park at 7003 Q Street is a combination amusement and water park. Cost: $13.95 for an all-day pass.
- The General Crook House Museum, on the Fort Omaha Campus of the Metropolitan Community College at Thirtieth and Fort streets, served as the residence of General George Crook during the 1870s' Indian Wars. Cost: $3.50.
- Henry Doorly Zoo at Deer Park Boulevard and Tenth Street. Cost: $5.75.
- Joslyn Art Museum, 2200 Dodge Street. Cost: $3.
- Peony Park, 8100 Cass Street, offers waterslides, a large pool and rides. Cost: About $13 per person.
- Western Heritage Museum, 801 South Tenth Street. Cost: $3.

Special Splurges

- Stay at least one night at the Omaha Marriott Hotel at 10220 Regency Circle. It has two heated pools, sauna, whirlpool and an exercise room. Cost: About $110 per night.
- In this same hotel you will find the Chardonnay Restaurant, an intimate and elegant dining room — just right for a romantic dinner. Cost: About $80 for two.

NORTH DAKOTA

Honeymoon No. 5 — Bismarck — Mandan — Missouri River

Romantic Appeal

- The Missouri River provides newlyweds with many things to do, including water skiing, canoeing, hiking, biking and riverboat cruising, all in a romantic honeymoon setting.

Free Attractions

- Bismarck Art Gallery, 422 East Front Avenue.
- Camp Hancock State Historic Site, First Street and Main Avenue in Bismarck.
- Former Governors' Mansion, 320 East Avenue.
- North Dakota Heritage Center on the Capitol Mall in Bismarck.
- The State Capitol at the end of North Sixth Street in Bismarck. This building contains a replica of the Liberty Bell, as well as the Roughrider Gallery.
- Take a walking tour of Bismarck and Mandan.
- Enjoy the festivities of Frontier Army Days in Mandan during the month of June, or Rodeo Days over the Fourth of July. Also, Winter Daze in February is a lot of fun.

Low-Cost Attractions

- Dakota Zoo, which adjoins Sertoma Riverside Park. Cost: $2.
- Fort Abraham Lincoln State Park includes the site of Fort Abraham Lincoln, the ruins of On-a-Slant Indian Village, a museum, hiking trails, scenic trolley rides, riverboat rides, camping and picnicking. Cost: $3 per car.
- Also on the grounds of Fort Abraham Lincoln State Park is Custer Home, a reconstruction of the Fort Abraham Lincoln commanding officer's quarters as it looked from 1873 to 1876. Costumed guides conduct tours. Cost: $3.25.

Special Splurges

- You can probably afford to spend your entire honeymoon at the Radisson Inn Bismarck at 800 South Third Street. It offers a great swimming pool, movies, saunas and whirlpool. Cost: About $65 per night.
- Caspar's East 40 Restaurant, at 1401 East Interchange Avenue in Bismarck, is a very trendy, popular local spot. The atmosphere is casual and fun. They specialize in prime rib and seafood. Cost: About $50 for two.

Honeymoon No. 6 — The Black Hills — Rapid City

Romantic Appeal

- Caverns, caves and canyons add to the excitement of a Black Hills honeymoon.

Free Attractions

- Walking tour to Rapid City.
- Black Hills Gold, 3 miles south of Rapid City at 5125 Highway 16 South, provides a close-up view of artisans making gold jewelry.
- Chapel in the Hills, on Chapel Lane in Rapid City, is a copy of the twelfth-century Borgund Stavkirke of Laerdal, Norway. There is also a museum that contains Norwegian antiques. This is a "must-see" for all you Scandinavians.
- Dahl Fine Arts Center, 713 Seventh Street, Rapid City, houses a 200-foot oil mural by Bernard Thomas that depicts scenes from 200 years of American history.
- South Dakota Air and Space Museum, located at Ellsworth Air Force Base off Highway 90 at exit 66.
- Landstrom's Original Black Hills Gold Creations, 405 Canal Street, Rapid City, provides a video presentation.
- Minnilusa Pioneer Museum, 515 West Boulevard in Halley Park, Rapid City.
- Museum of Geology, Administration Building, School of Mines and Technology, 1 mile east on Highway 79, contains rocks, minerals and ores from around the world, and fossils from the Badlands.
- Sioux Indian Museum, 515 West Boulevard, next to the Minnilusa Pioneer Museum, exhibits the works of Sioux and other Native American artisans.
- Take a scenic drive along Skyline Drive, extending southwest out of Rapid City. It offers views of the Black Hills and prairies.
- Two miles southwest of Keystone via highways 16A and 244 is Mount Rushmore National Memorial, featuring the colossal sculpted heads of four presidents, plus a visitor center that shows a film and presents a program. Keystone is only about 6 miles southeast of Rapid City.

Low-Cost Attractions

- Beautiful Rushmore Cave, off Highway 44 in Rapid City, has a series of chambers and a large cave room with a colorful variety of logomites, stalactites, stalagmites, and dog-tooth and nailhead spar crystal. There is also a museum, and you can bring your own picnic to enjoy. Cost: $5.50.
- Crystal Cave Park, on Crystal Cave Road in Rapid City, is a well-lighted cavern with almost every type of cave formation found in the Black Hills. Cost: $5.25.

- Sitting Bull Crystal Caverns, off Highway 16 in Rapid City, has a rare calcite crystal called dogtooth spar. Cost: $5.
- Bear Country U.S.A., 8 miles south of Rapid City on Highway 16, is a drive-through wildlife park. Cost: $7.
- Black Hills Petrified Forest, on Elk Creek Road, Rapid City. Cost: $4.50.
- Black Hills Reptile Gardens, on Mount Rushmore Road, Rapid City, features the Sky Dome reptile house. Cost: $7.
- Marine Life Aquarium, 3 miles south of Rapid City on Highway 16, presents performing dolphins, seals and sea lions. Cost: $7.50.
- If you're honeymooning during the summer, you may want to order tickets for the "Black Hills Passion Play" performed in nearby Spearfish. Tickets can be reserved by calling (605)642-2646. Performances are every Sunday, Tuesday and Thursday during June, July and August. Cost: $5 to $12.

Special Splurges

- The Rushmore Plaza Holiday Inn, at 505 North Fifth Street in Rapid City, has an atrium with a waterfall, plus movies, heated indoor pool, sauna, whirlpools and an exercise room. Cost: About $90 per night.
- You must have at least one meal at Windows on the ninth floor of the First Federal Plaza Building in Rapid City. The dining room offers an excellent view of the area. Cost: About $50 for two.

OKLAHOMA

HONEYMOON NO. 7 — TULSA — SAND SPRINGS

Romantic Appeal

- A night at Rogers and Hammersteins play *Oklahoma!*, performed under the stars.
- A romantic walk through the Tulsa Gardens, with profuse dogwoods.
- An exciting ride on a giant roller coaster.

Free Attractions

- A visit to River Parks is a must. Something is always going on, from one of their 25 festivals to performances on their floating stage. There are also many trails for hiking along the east and west banks of the Arkansas River.
- A walking tour of Tulsa, including several restored buildings at the Williams Center, which is bounded by Cincinnati and Boulder avenues, and Archer and Third streets.
- Enjoy the festivities that accompany Tulsa's annual events, such as the Tulsa Indian Art Festival, held in March, the Gilcrease Rendezvous every June, the Greenwood Jazz Festival in August, the Chili Cookoff and Bluegrass Festival in September, Oktoberfest

in October, Mayfest, a five-day celebration held in May, and the Concert on the Ice, presented by the Tulsa Philharmonic Orchestra on the Sunday that follows Thanksgiving.

- Thomas Gilcrease Museum, off Highway 64/51, exhibits oil paintings, sculpture and Indian artifacts.
- A walking tour of Sand Springs, overlooking the Arkansas River, just west of downtown Tulsa.
- Tulsa Gardens, 2435 South Peoria Avenue, Tulsa.

Low-Cost Attractions

- Bell's Amusement Park, 3900 East Twenty-first Street, Tulsa. Cost: Gate admission — $1; full-day package — $12, plus individual tickets for miniature golf — $2.
- Big Splash Water Park, 4707 East Twenty-first Street, Tulsa, features a seven-story waterslide. Cost: $13.55.
- Oxley Nature Center in Mohawk Park at 6700 East Mohawk Boulevard, Tulsa. Cost: $1 on weekends, otherwise it is free.
- Philbrook Museum of Art, at 2727 Rockford Road in Tulsa, is an elaborate Italian Renaissance-style villa set on 23 acres. The museum houses permanent art collections. Cost: $3.
- Tulsa Zoo in Mohawk Park, Tulsa. Cost: $3.
- Discoveryland! on Forty-first Street in Sand Springs provides an outdoor amphitheater where the Rogers and Hammerstein play *Oklahoma!* is performed under the stars. There are real horses and wagons, a real surrey with the fringe on top, and a barbecue dinner that precedes the show at extra cost. Cost of the performance: $12.

Special Splurges

- The Westin Hotel Williams Center is a four-star hotel. Try this one on weekends when the rates are lower. It has a couple of swimming pools, a whirlpool and movies. There is a fee for the health club and ice skating. The hotel boasts a trendy nightclub as well. Cost: About $65 per night on Friday, Saturday and Sunday; about $165 per night Monday through Thursday.
- The Warren Duck Club, located in the Doubletree Hotel at 6110 South Yale Avenue, is a formal restaurant with a relaxing view. Here is a chance for you to dress up. Cost: About $60 for two.

GREAT ESCAPES ON A BUDGET

CHAPTER 20

ALOHA!

Affordable Hawaiian Honeymoons

Hawaii is for lovers. From swaying palm trees, to fragrant flower leis, to the starry nights, the Hawaiian Islands offer a honeymoon filled with memories and dreams of paradise found. There is the gentle trade wind that carries the scent of flowers, the sparkling sea that hosts spectacular sunsets and rainbows, and the cascading waterfall that provides nature's harmonic symphony. I have traveled to Hawaii seven times on a variety of budgets and, in my opinion, you can definitely have a fabulous time on a small budget. Hawaii is a "no-fail" destination and one of my favorite vacation spots.

I have selected the island of Oahu as the obvious choice for an affordable honeymoon destination. According to a recent survey taken by *Bride's* magazine, the average expenditure for a Hawaiian honeymoon is $4,500. However, I want you to have a "fabulous, romantic and affordable" one for less than $1,500, which is why I recommend Oahu, the most affordable island.

Oahu has many free attractions, reasonable hotel rates and restaurants and, best of all, lower airfares from the mainland. I think the "travel snobs" who complain that Oahu is too crowded and commercialized probably checked into a Waikiki hotel, sat on Waikiki beach, shopped on the strip in front of the hotels, and never rented a car to see the sights. Trust me, Oahu is loaded with secluded coves and beaches, pineapple plantations, and more un-crowded attractions than you can cover in a week. The key is to rent a car and have a daily itinerary.

Now, let's see how you can hold the total cost of your Hawaiian honeymoon to less than $1,500. First of all, this total must include your airfare, hotel, meals, transfers, car rental, tips and spending money. The best way to achieve this is to purchase a package deal.

PACKAGE DEALS

There are many group packages to Hawaii, the most reasonable of which are to Oahu, arriving at the airport in Honolulu. These packages are offered through travel agencies, airlines, and independent tour companies that specialize in Hawaiian vacations. Here are some ideas:

- PLEASANT HAWAIIAN HOLIDAYS
  With this tour company you can stay under $1,500 for a six-day, five-night honeymoon, depending on the hotel you select and what zone they will be flying you from on the

mainland. In addition to the airfare, most of these packages include flower lei greeting, round-trip transfers, baggage tips and handling, Dollar Rent a Car and optional extras, such as the Dole Cannery tour, continental breakfast, and *Memories of Hawaii* book. Inquire at your local travel agency.

- TWA GETAWAY VACATIONS
  TWA offers what they call Hawaii On Sale with trips starting at $389 per person, which includes round-trip airfare from San Francisco, five nights at a Waikiki hotel, lei greeting, hotel taxes and transfers. Call them at (800)GETAWAY.

- DELTA DREAM VACATIONS
  Delta offers several Waikiki packages, starting at $399 per person, including five nights at the Outrigger Maile Sky Court Hotel, round-trip airfare, airport transfers, baggage handling and gratuities. Call them at (800)872-7786.

- EMPIRE TOURS
  Empire offers airfare, plus five nights at a hotel in Waikiki, flower lei greeting, transfers, a breakfast and the hotel tax, all starting at $369 per person from San Francisco. Call (800)833-3333.

- CONTINENTAL GREAT VACATIONS
  Continental Airlines, in conjunction with American Express as tour operator, offers packages to Waikiki that include airfare, five nights at a Waikiki hotel, transfers, lei greeting and all taxes, starting at $482 per person. Call them at (800)YES-AMEX.

A La Carte Planning

You may be able to design your Hawaiian honeymoon for even less than the package prices by picking and choosing your own airfare, accommodations, car rentals and restaurants.

AIRLINE FARES

Use all the ideas from chapter 3, plus ads in the travel sections of your local and West Coast Sunday newspapers. You can find copies of the *San Francisco Examiner* and the *Los Angeles Times* at your local library. Here are a few of the places you can call to purchase round-trip airfare from San Francisco to Honolulu for about $240 per person (some restrictions apply):

- Cheap Tickets, Inc. — (800)234-4522
- Hawaii Reservation Center — (800)366-0455
- Airline Ticket Express — (408)245-5090

The only round-trip airfare I found less than this was $219 (San Francisco to Honolulu) through:

- Suntrips (415)394-7700

In addition to the West Coast to Honolulu airfare, you will, of course, need to fly from your home state to the West Coast. Again, use the cost-saving suggestions in chapter 3 to book the lowest fare available. Airfares change daily, but here is a general idea of round-trip fares from various cities to San Francisco:

- From Chicago   About $300
- From Dallas   About $230
- From Miami   About $500
- From New York City   About $320
- From St. Louis   About $280
- From New Orleans   About $360
- From Washington, D.C.   About $350
- From Atlanta   About $270

ACCOMMODATIONS

The next item on your à la carte menu is your accommodations. You will need to look over your *Mobile Tour Guide* or your *AAA Tour Book* for more ideas, but here is a list of hotels on Oahu that cost less than $99 per night:

- Aston Hotels—There are five Astons.
  (800)445-6633 or (800)922-7866   Cost: $63 to $85
- Coconut Plaza Hotel, 450 Lewers Street, Honolulu.
  (800)882-9696   Cost: $70 to $80 per night
- Continental Surf Hotel, 2426 Kuhio Avenue, Honolulu.
  (800)367-5004   Cost: $63 to $73 per night
- Hawaiiana Hotel, 260 Beach Walk, Honolulu.
  (800)628-3098   Cost: $85 per night
- Ilima Hotel, 445 Nohonani Street, Honolulu.
  (808)923-5200   Cost: $77 to $89 per night
- Malihini Hotel, 217 Saratoga Road, Honolulu
  (800)367-9644   Cost: $45 to $48 per night
- Outrigger Hotels—There are 16 Outriggers.
  (800)733-7777   Cost: $45 to $90
  (Many of these hotels include the use of a Geo Metro rental car—ask.)

- Queen Kapiolani Hotel, 1150 South King Street, Honolulu.
  (800)533-6970   Cost: $92 per night
- Waikiki Gateway Hotel, 2070 Kalakaua Avenue, Honolulu.
  (800)633-8799   Cost: $55 to $80 per night
- Waikiki Sand Villa Hotel, 2375 Ala Wai Boulevard, Honolulu.
  (800)247-1903   Cost: $56 to $70 per night

Here are three reasonably priced bed-and-breakfasts, none of which are located in Honolulu. They require a rental car to get around the island of Oahu.

- Alii Bluffs Windward, 46-251 Ikiiki Street, Kaneohe.
  (808)235-1124   Cost: $50 to $55 per night
- Tutu's Place, 1120 Kamahele Street, Kailua.
  (808)261-0975   Cost: $50 per night
- Pacific-Hawaii Bed & Breakfast, 970 N. Kalaheo Avenue, Kailua.
  (800)999-6026   Cost: $45 to $95 per night

You might also want to look in the travel sections of big city newspapers for private condos, homes or cottages for rent. Here are a couple of examples, just to give you an idea of what is being advertised:

Aloha Towers, Waikiki, vacation condos, 30 units in 14 buildings. Rates: $65 for a studio.

Waikiki Penthouse — Full view of Diamond Head & Ocean. Sunny, remodeled, one bedroom. Extras. $550/week.

DINING

One advantage of honeymooning on Oahu is the great selection of reasonably priced restaurants. Here are just a few suggestions. Perry's Smorgy Restaurants has three locations: the Outrigger Waikiki Hotel, the Coral Seas Hotel, and 2380 Kuhio Avenue. They are all-you-can-eat and cost about $4 for breakfast, $5.50 for lunch and $8 for dinner. Spaghetti! Spaghetti! (2233 Kalakaua Avenue) is an all-you-can-eat spaghetti buffet and salad bar for $5. There are about a dozen Subway Salads & Sandwiches — great for take-out picnics on the beach. Prices start at about $2 for sub sandwiches. The Original Pancake House is located at 1221 Kapiolani Boulevard and in the Waikiki Marina Hotel. They have omelets starting at $3.50. They also serve lunches at reasonable prices, including hot sandwiches in the $3 to $4 range.

There are also dozens of affordable ethnic restaurants scattered around as well; you will have fun ferreting out the best prices and ambience. One of the nicest surprises is the lunch buffet at Maiko at the Ilikai Hotel where for $8.50 you may eat all the crab, sushi, sukiyaki, salad and dessert you want.

CAR RENTALS

If you stay in the general Honolulu/Waikiki/Ala Moana part of Oahu, you won't need to rent a car at all because of the convenient, affordable transportation. First of all, there is The Bus (the local bus company, so named because that is what the tourists always called it). This reasonable form of transportation runs all over the Honolulu area and only costs 60 cents. Taxis are also reasonable and accessible; it should never take you more than five minutes to flag one down. They charge $2.60 for the first mile and $1.40 for each additional mile. You will definitely want to rent a car for the outlying areas of Oahu, including day trips to Makaha Beach, Sunset Beach, Sea Life Park, the Polynesian Cultural Center, pineapple plantation tours, Waimea Falls and all the other attractions on the north and east shores of the island. The beaches, Falls and plantation tours are free. These are typical car rental prices on the island of Oahu:

- Budget (800)527-7000   Cost: $87 a week
- Alamo (800)GO-ALAMO   Cost: $95 a week
- Avis (800)831-8000   Cost: $99 a week
- Hertz (800)654-3131   Cost: $99 a week

All these prices are for their subcompact cars, often a Geo Metro. Their daily rates run about $27.

FREE OR LOW-COST ATTRACTIONS

There is so much to do on the island of Oahu that you can't take it all in during one trip; you'll want to come back many times, as my husband and I do. Here are some of our favorite attractions that cost under $10:

- Dole Cannery Square, Honolulu (shops, exhibits, cafes, tour). Cost: $5.
- Foster Botanical Garden, Honolulu. Cost: $1.
- Honolulu Zoo, right in Waikiki. Cost: $3.
- Kodak Hula Show, Honolulu (in the Waikiki Shell, right off Waikiki Beach). Cost: Free.
- Royal Hawaiian Band Concerts, usually at the Iolani Palace Grounds in Honolulu at Friday noon and at Kapiolani Park every Sunday at 2 P.M. Cost: Free.
- U.S.S. *Arizona* Memorial, Pearl Harbor, Honolulu. There is a museum, film and shuttle trip to the memorial. Cost: Free.
- *Free* festivals (Hawaiians *love* to celebrate):
  —Aloha Week—September or October
  —Kamehameha Day—June 11
  —Cherry Blossom Festival—February to April
  —Narcissus Festival—January or February

—Lei Day—May 1
—Celebration of Kites—March
—Festival of the Pacific—June
—Prince Lot Hula Festival—July

- Honolulu Academy of Arts, 900 South Beretania Street. Cost: Free.
- Enjoy Kapiolani Park (between Waikiki Beach and Diamond Head), a 300-acre park that contains an aquarium, golf driving range, archery field, bandstand, tennis courts and picnic sites. Cost: Free.
- You will find, if you're just a tiny bit clever, that you can enjoy an entire luau without having to pay the $35 per person fare. Most of these Hawaiian parties take place on the ocean side of major hotels, and can be seen from the adjoining beach.

SPECIAL SPLURGES

- Polynesian Cultural Center, on Highway 83 around the other side of the island from Waikiki, is a 35-acre park that has exhibition areas, pageants, cultural presentations, and an extravaganza called "This is Polynesia," a 90-minute show featuring a cast of more than 125 islanders. Cost: Admission with buffet dinner and show—$39 per person; admission only—$20 per person.
- Glider rides over the northwest coast of Oahu depart from Dillingham Airfield, west of Mokuleia off Highway 930. Cost: $60 per couple.
- Go see the Don Ho show at the Hilton Hawaiian Village Dome Showroom. Cocktail show: $24 per person.
- Sea Life Park on Highway 72 at Makapuu Point is a 62-acre oceanarium offering shows and exhibits. Cost: $14.95 per person.
- The Sheraton's Spectacular Polynesian Revue at the Ainahu Showroom of the Princess Kaiulani Hotel would be a special treat for you. Cost: $44.50 per person.
- Enjoy a meal at Maile Restaurant at the Kahala Hilton (on a day when you have a rental car). The elegant atmosphere will give you a chance to do the "dress-up thing." Cost: About $120 for two.

HELPFUL HINTS FOR TRAVELING TO HAWAII

- Don't let anyone, including a travel agent, pressure you into believing you must spend more than $1,500 on a Hawaiian honeymoon. Travel agents are used to arranging pricier trips to Hawaii, usually encompassing two or more islands, so you'll have to convince them you know what you're talking about.

- Write for free visitor information from:
Hawaii Visitors Bureau
2270 Kalakaua Avenue
Honolulu, HI 96815
- Go to your local library and check out a copy of *Hawaii on $60 a Day*, Frommer's budget travel guide. His "$60 a day" is per person for lodging and three meals.
- Follow the advice of noted dermatologist, Dr. Norman Goldstein, who says you can still get a tan while protecting your skin if you use a sunscreen with an 8 SPF (skin protection factor). Don't lather yourselves in oil without sunscreen; it will only roast you like a pig on a spit.
- Don't be afraid of the small friendly lizard called a Gecko. You *want* your hotel room to have these cute little guys — they eat the cockroaches and they won't hurt you in the slightest. (By the way, you'll never see a snake in Hawaii — they are taboo.)
- When you're looking for a restroom remember, "Wahine" means woman and "Kane" means man.
- Winter temperatures are in the high 70s; summer, in the mid-80s. Therefore, light-weight, casual clothing is the thing. Women can always wear a muumuu, the all-purpose local dress; men may be required to don a sports jacket for certain formal occasions.
- Whatever else you pack, be sure to bring at least one pair of broken-in, comfortable walking shoes.
- Sorry, the law of the land allows no public nudity, just in case you were wanting to shed part of your swimsuit.
- Don't take the ocean for granted. You are advised never to swim alone; never turn your back on the surf; never swim where there are "No Swimming" signs. Also, watch out for coral in the water. My favorite beach for swimming is the one at the Hale Koa Hotel (a military hotel at Fort DeRussy). The beach is open to the public and doesn't seem to have the coral that some of the other beaches do. You can walk to this beach from the main part of Waikiki.

If you choose Hawaii, there's no way you can go wrong! Have a wonderful Polynesian honeymoon!

CHAPTER 21

OH, CANADA!
Affordable Canadian Honeymoons

Whether you live in Canada or the United States, a Canadian honeymoon definitely qualifies as "fabulous, romantic and affordable." The total expense can easily stay under $800, including spending money. See if one of these seven Canadian honeymoons appeals to you.

BRITISH COLUMBIA
HONEYMOON NO. 1 — VANCOUVER

Romantic Appeal
- From the Fraser River to English Bay, Vancouver is lavishly sprinkled with greenery and ringed by the Pacific Ocean, offering newlyweds natural beauty amid a cosmopolitan honeymoon setting.

Free Attractions
- Walking tour along Granville Street near Granville Square.
- Hang out at Granville Square and people-watch; this square is also a perfect vantage point for the port activities, including the arrival of seaplanes, barges, tugboats, ferries and the SeaBus.
- Take a driving tour to Simon Fraser University atop Burnaby Mountain for an overall view of the city of Vancouver, the sea and adjacent mountains.
- Hike along the designated paths in any of Vancouver's city parks; use their swimming pools, putting greens, golf courses and lawn bowling greens.
- Swim in English Bay (take Beach Avenue from downtown).
- Enjoy Vancouver's festivals, including the Rain Festival the first Sunday in April, the Folkfest in June, the Vancouver Sea Festival and Bathtub Race in mid-July, the Pacific National Exhibition in late August and Oktoberfest held every October. In case you're in Vancouver during December, you'll enjoy the Christmas Carol Ship which leads a flotilla around the harbor.
- Deer Lake Park, 6450 Deer Lake Avenue, has gardens, an art gallery, a model steam railway and Sunday afternoon artist fairs.
- B.C. Pavilion in Exhibition Park, between Renfrew and Cassiar Streets, contains the British Columbia Sports Hall of Fame.

- Lynn Canyon Park, Lynn Valley Road in North Vancouver, is a parkway with paths and walks, a natural swimming pool, a fishing pool, and a suspension bridge spanning a waterfall and the canyon.
- North Shore Museum and Art Gallery, 333 Chesterfield Avenue, in North Vancouver.

Low-Cost Attractions

- Take the Aqua Bus to Granville Island, departing daily from Burrard Bridge. Cost: About $2.50 per person.
- Enjoy the nightlife with lounges that offer everything from rock 'n' roll to jazz. Try the Panoroma Roof at the Vancouver Hotel, the Cloud 9 at the Sheraton Landmark, or Humphrey's at the top of the Ramada Renaissance.
- Playland Amusement Park, at Renfrew, East Hastings and Cassiar streets, has rides, games, miniature golf and a large roller coaster. Cost: $5.
- Grouse Mountain, 6400 Nancy Greene Way, North Vancouver, offers a panoramic view of the city. Ride the aerial tramway. Cost: $12.95.
- Harbour Centre Complex, 555 West Hastings Street, has an observation deck offering a view of the city. Ride the skylift elevator. Cost: $5.
- H.R. Macmillan Planetarium, 1100 Chestnut Street, presents laser light shows and astronomy programs. Cost: $4.75.
- Vancouver Public Aquarium at Stanley Park, on the downtown peninsula, exhibits more than 9,000 marine animals. Cost: $8.
- Vancouver Art Gallery, 750 Hornby Street, houses major paintings by Canadian artists. Cost: $4.25.
- Vancouver Museum, 1100 Chestnut Street. Cost: $5.

Special Splurges

- Take a six-hour round-trip on the steam locomotive Royal Hudson; you will see magnificent scenery between North Vancouver and Squamish. The train departs North Vancouver daily at 9:30 A.M. Cost: $24.
- Take a one-and-a-half-hour harbor tour aboard the sternwheeler *Constitution* Harbour Ferries, Ltd., has schedule information by phone: (604)687-9558. Cost: $18.
- The M.V. *Britannia* departs downtown Vancouver for a scenic cruise along the coast to Squamish. Call (604)687-9558 for schedule information. Cost: $45.
- Stay at the Sands Motor Hotel, 1755 Davis Street, one block from English Bay Beach. Cost: About $75 per night.
- Have lunch at Trader Vic's in the Westin Bayshore Hotel. Trader Vic's are known worldwide for their romantic ambience. Cost: About $75 for two.

SASKATCHEWAN

HONEYMOON NO. 2 — PRINCE ALBERT

Romantic Appeal

- This is the nature lovers' ideal honeymoon setting, from its sandy beaches to its conifer forests and resident wildlife. What a wonderful spot for newlyweds to relax and enjoy each other after all the stress and hustle of the wedding.

Free Attractions

- Enjoy Prince Albert's festivals, including the Prince Albert Exhibition from late July to early August and the Winter Festival every February.
- Diefenbaker House Museum, 246 Nineteenth Street, West, Prince Albert.
- Little Red River Park on Highway 55; take the scenic drive that follows the north bank of the North Saskatchewan River. This park offers picnicking in the summer and winter sports in the winter.
- Enjoy Prince Albert National Park, 50 miles north of the city of Prince Albert, where you can fish, swim, hike, bicycle and mingle with the wildlife.
- Join a free car caravan hosted by the park naturalists in Prince Albert National Park.

Low-Cost Attractions

- There are dozens of low-cost activities in Prince Albert National Park, including boating, canoeing, tennis, bowling, volleyball, golf and paddle-wheeler tours.
- Historical Museum, 10 River Street East at Central Avenue in Prince Albert. Cost: $1.50.
- Lund Wildlife Exhibit, River Street West, Prince Albert. Cost: $3.

Special Splurges

- Enjoy Greek ribs, the specialty at Venice House, 1498 Central Avenue in Prince Avenue. Cost: About $40 for two.

MANITOBA

HONEYMOON NO. 3 — WINNIPEG

Romantic Appeal

- This honeymoon setting will keep newlyweds entertained with its big-city glamour and excitement.

Free Attractions

- Take a walking tour of historic Winnipeg's Exchange District, near Portage Avenue and Main Street. Depart from the Manitoba Museum of Man and Nature.
- Enjoy Winnipeg's festivals, including the Festival du Voyageur every February, the Red

River Exhibition in late June, the Winnipeg Folk Festival in July, the Folklorama in August, and Oktoberfest in early September.

- Saint Norbert Provincial Heritage Park, 40 Turnbull Drive in Winnipeg, has 17 acres on the banks of the Red River with restored farmhouses.
- Seven Oaks House, Main Street on Rupertsland Boulevard, Winnipeg.
- Aquatic Hall of Fame and Museum, in the Pan Am Building at 25 Poseidon Bay, Winnipeg.
- Assiniboine Park, Wellington Crescent, Winnipeg, has a miniature railway, a conservatory, pool, fountain, gallery, picnicking, bicycling, horse and buggy rides in the summer, or ice skating and sleigh rides in the winter.
- Living Prairie Museum and Nature Preserve, 2795 Ness Ave., Winnipeg, offers exhibits, nature talks and hikes.

Low-Cost Attractions

- Take a paddlewheel *River Rouge* tour of Winnipeg. Docked near Water Avenue at the foot of the Provencher Bridge, the *River Rouge* offers daytime and evening cruises on the Assiniboine and Red rivers. Cost: $9 and $10 per person.
- Winnipeg has become known for its diversified nightlife, from quiet piano bars to flashing lights. Try the Crystal Casino in Hotel Fort Garry for its European-style atmosphere or the Palomino Club for country-western dancing.
- Winnipeg Art Gallery, 300 Memorial Boulevard, Winnipeg. Cost: $3.
- Western Canada Aviation Museum, 958 Ferry Road, Hanger T2, has a collection of airplanes, an education center and a flight deck. Cost: $2.50.
- Dalnavert, 61 Carlton Street, Winnipeg, is a restored Victorian home. Cost: $3.
- Grant's Old Mill on Portage and Booth Avenues, Winnipeg, is a reconstructed log mill. Cost: $1.
- Manitoba Museum of Man and Nature, Main Street and Rupert Avenue, Winnipeg. Cost: $3.50.
- Manitoba Planetarium, located at the Manitoba Museum of Man and Nature, presents shows in the Star Theatre. Cost: $3.

Special Splurges

- You may be able to spend your entire honeymoon at the Country Resort by Carlson in nearby Gimli where you will have your own private balcony with a beach or lake view, fishing, two heated pools plus swimming at the beach, sauna and whirlpool. Cost: About $70 per night.
- You can dress up for an exquisite dinner at the four-star Market Grill in Holiday Inn Winnipeg Downtown. Cost: About $75 for two.

Honeymoon No. 4 — The City of Quebec

Romantic Appeal

- The city of Quebec provides a French-European honeymoon setting, complete with its tempting cuisine, dangerously narrow streets and regally carved bluffs — perfect for the couple who wanted Paris but couldn't afford it.

Free Attractions

- Enjoy a walking tour of the historic section of Old Quebec, within the walls of Upper Town.
- Artillery Park National Historic Site, within the walls at Porte St.-Jean, is a fascinating place to explore with its old arsenal foundry, exhibit depictions, relief map and officers' quarters.
- Hotel-Dieu Augustines Museum, 32 rue Charlevoix, marks the site of North America's first hospital, built in 1639 by French nuns.
- Founded in 1824, the Library of the Literary and Historical Society of Quebec, at 44 rue St.-Stanislas, boasts a famous collection of memorabilia.
- Chevalier House, 60 rue du Marche Champlain, houses a gallery with changing exhibits.
- Enjoy one of Quebec's three major annual events: Carnaval de Quebec in February, Quebec International Summer Festival in July, or Expo-Quebec, which runs for 10 days in late August.

Low-Cost Attractions

- The Citadel, on the cap Diamant promontory (entrance is off rue St.-Louis) is famous for its ceremonial guard changes daily at 10 A.M. Cost: $3.
- Dufferin Terrace, next to Chateau Frontenac, offers a spectacular view of Old Lower Town and the St. Lawrence. You can get there by climbing 61 steps or riding an enclosed cliffside elevator. Cost: The elevator is 85 cents.
- Museum of Civilization, 85 rue Dalhousie, is a landmark of modern architecture with a series of galleries that present changing exhibits. Cost: $4.
- Seminary Museum, 9 rue de l'Universite, is an old university boarding school with museum items acquired by priests during their nineteenth-century travels. Cost: $2.
- Aquarium, 1675 avenue du Parc, includes seal shows. Cost: $3.75.
- Quebec Museum, 1 avenue Wolf-Montcalm in National Battlefields Park, contains a large collection of fine arts. Cost: $5.
- Quebec Zoo, 8191 avenue du Zoo. Cost: $5.75.
- Enjoy Quebec's nightlife with its array of entertainment. Try Cabaret at Loews le Con-

corde or Bar L'Imprevu at Auberge des Gouverneurs, 690 rue St.-Cyrille East. Also, get a copy of the entertainment guide, *Quebec Magazine*.

Special Splurges

- Take a cruise of the Quebec area aboard the MK/V *Louis Jolliet*, Quebec City Cruises, 10 rue Dalhousie. There is a one-hour harbor cruise or a one-and-a-half-hour cruise to the ile d'Orleans. Cost: From $13 to $23.25 per person.
- Stay at Le Chateau de Pierre, 17 avenue Ste.-Genevieve, a converted English mansion with a walled garden courtyard. Located in Old Quebec Uppertown, it is within walking distance of all the historical spots as well as better restaurants and shopping. Ask for their honeymoon suite. Cost: About $85 per night.
- Enjoy Sunday brunch at the renowned Le Champlain Dining Room in Le Chateau Frontenanc, overlooking the boardwalk and St. Lawrence River. You can dress up for this spot, which has a refined atmosphere and superb menu. Cost: About $60 for two for Sunday brunch.

ATLANTIC PROVINCES

HONEYMOON NO. 5 — CAVENDISH — PRINCE EDWARD ISLAND

Route

- Prince Edward Island is accessible by ferry from New Brunswick and Nova Scotia.
- If arriving by ferry from Nova Scotia, take Highway 1 northwest to Highway 7, then northwest on Highway 7 to Cavendish.
- If arriving by ferry from New Brunswick, take Highway 1A northwest to Highway 6, then northeast on Highway 6 to Cavendish.

Romantic Appeal

- Prince Edward Island, nicknamed the Playground Province, offers water sports galore, including swimming, sailing, canoeing, scuba diving and wind surfing. Add to this a little "go-see-do," and the honeymooners will welcome a soothing soak in their own private whirlpool tub each evening.

Free Attractions

- Walking tour of Cavendish, affectionately described in the popular book, *Anne of Green Gables*.
- Green Gables House, west of Highway 13 on Highway 6, part of Prince Edward Island National Park, offers tours.

Low-Cost Attractions

- Cap'n Bart's Adventure Park, a theme park on Highway 6, offers swimming, miniature

golf, boating and kayaking. There are also several museums. Cost: $5.95.
- The Enchanted Castle, also on Highway 6, offers miniature golf and King Tut's Tomb and Treasures, containing a full-size reproduction of the Egyptian king's tomb. Cost: The Enchanted Castle — $3.75; King Tut's Tomb and Treasures — $3.75.
- Prince Edward Island Marine Aquarium, Highway 6, Cavendish. Cost: $3.75.
- Rainbow Valley, at the junction of Highways 6 and 13, has picnic sites, a waterslide and boating. Cost: $8.50.
- Ripley's Believe It or Not! Museum, on Highway 6, Cavendish. Cost: $5.75.
- Royal Atlantic Wax Museum, junction of Highways 6 and 13, has life-size models from Madame Tussaud's of England. Cost: $4.60.
- Sandspit, Highway 6 in Cavendish, offers an amusement park, plus an old-fashioned carnival, miniature golf and a slide. Cost: Admission is free, but each ride costs from $1.30 to $3.25.

Special Splurges
- Stay at least one night at Sundance Cottages on Route 6, Rural Route 1, in Cavendish. Your cottage will have a large sundeck that overlooks the ocean. There is a heated pool and bicycles are available for rent. Ask for a cottage with is own private whirlpool tub. Cost: About $100 per night.
- Enjoy a lobster dinner at St. Ann's Church Lobster Suppers on Route 224 in Cavendish, featuring live entertainment. Cost: About $40 for two.

Helpful Hints for Traveling to Canada

- You do not need a passport to enter Canada or to return to the United States, however, proof of citizenship must be carried: A birth, baptismal or voter's certificate will usually do. You may also need proof of residence.
- If driving your car into Canada, you will need a vehicle registration card. If the car isn't registered in your name, you will need written permission from the owner for use of the car in Canada. If you have a rental car, you will need to show a copy of your rental contract. You will also need a Canadian Non-Resident Inter-Provincial Motor Vehicle Liability Insurance card from your insurance company.
- All prices and fees in this chapter are in Canadian dollars; don't try to pay in American dollars. It is best to change your U.S. funds into Canadian traveler's checks at a bank before entering the country.

CHAPTER 22

SOUTH OF THE BORDER

Affordable Mexican Honeymoons

A Mexican honeymoon is one of the best travel bargains around. In fact, it would win first prize in a biggest bang for the buck contest. Here's the way to afford those hot, white sand beaches, warm ocean waters, and sizzling all-night parties—fiesta-style!

Unless you plan to bicycle or to drop in via parachute, you'll probably travel to Mexico one of these three ways: drive a car, fly or take a cruise. All three ways are affordable on a small budget. If you drive to your destination, your total honeymoon expense can easily be held under $500; if you fly, less than $1,000; and if you cruise, about $1,500, including your tips and spending money.

Let's take a look at some of the package deals that combine airfare and lodging.

PACKAGE DEALS

These packages are offered through travel agencies, airlines, and independent tour companies that specialize in Mexican vacations. Remember to check the travel section of your local Sunday newspapers to find the most affordable packages from your home state. Here are some typical packages to give you an idea of what is being offered; however, many of these trips may cost even less from your part of the country.

- EMPIRE TOURS
  This company offers a four-night, five-day trip to Mazatlan for $264 per person. The trip is via Alaska Airlines and the package includes the airfare, round-trip transfers, hotel accommodations, hotel tax and a little cruise. There are restrictions that must be met, and the price is good only for a Sunday departure. They also offer a similar three-night, four-day trip to Puerto Vallarta for $284 per person. Call (800)833-3333.
- SUNTRIPS
  You'll choose from among several trips to Mexico when you travel with Suntrips. Choices include a three-night, four-day package to Cancun for $409 per person; a three-night, four-day package to Puerto Vallarta for $269; and a seven-night, eight-day trip to Mazatlan for only $329. All their package deals have restrictions and are subject to seasonal surcharge and capacity control. Suntrips' packages include hotel and airfare (via a private, chartered airline). Call (415)394-7700.

- MEXICANA AIRLINES

Cancun

Plaza del Sol

$419 (four days, three nights)

Fiesta Americana Condesa

$598 (four days, three nights)

Puerto Vallarta

Costa Alegre

$284 (four days, three nights)

Hyatt Coral Grand

$378 (four days, three nights)

Mazatlan

Azteca Inn

$254 (four days, three nights)

Camino Real

$389 (four days, three nights)

Los Cabos

Posada Real

$296 (four days, three nights)

Finisterra

$381 (four days, three nights)

All of these prices are per person and include round-trip airfare on Mexicana Airlines, accommodations, and round-trip transfers between the airport and hotel. They do not include United States or Mexican departure taxes (fees charged when you leave a country) or customs fees (charged on goods brought into the United States from Mexico). There are also the normal restrictions and prices that are subject to change. For example, surcharges may be possible after a certain date. Empire Tours arranges all these Mexicana Airlines package trips; call them at the number given above.

- AMERICAN AIRLINES FLY A'AWAY VACATIONS

Acapulco

Depending on the quality of the hotel, prices start at about $321 per person for a three-night, four-day package deal. This particular deal includes a stay at the Radisson Paraiso Acapulco, a very nice hotel right on the beach that has three restaurants, a pool, and a beach snack bar. All American Airlines' Acapulco packages include round-trip airfare, hotel accommodations, round-trip airport transfers, 10 percent hotel room tax, $6 international transportation tax, and $7 federal/health inspection fees.

While in Acapulco, you'll find American Airlines packages offer three optional tours, well worth the money:

City Tour (three-and-a-half hours) Cost: $15

Yacht Cruise Around the Bay With Buffet Dinner (three-and-a-half hours) Cost: $47

Cliff Divers by Night with Dinner (four-and-a-half hours) Cost: $44

Puerto Vallara

Depending on the quality of the hotel, American Airlines' Puerto Vallarta packages start at about $351 per person for a four-day, three-night stay and include airfare, hotel, transfers and all taxes. While in Puerto Vallarta, American Airlines offers these two optional tours:

Tropical Tour (five hours) Cost: $15

Cielito Lindo Trimaran (six hours) Cost: $39

Cancun

These packages start at $399 per person for four days and three nights and have all the same inclusions as the first two destinations, with these three optional tours:

Tulum Xel Ha (half day) Cost: $33

Suntour Isla Mujeres (half day) Cost: $47

Chichen Itza (full day) Cost: $62

Cozumel

For a four-day, three-night package, prices start at $473 per person and include all the same goodies as the others.

Mexico City

Spend four days and three nights on a package trip starting at $351 per person, including all the same amenities as the Acapulco and Puerto Vallarta packages.

Guadalajara

A four-day, three-night package starts at $399 per person, again all-inclusive.

Add-on airfares

All of these package prices are effective from certain airports in the United States and depend on the destination, as well. To determine the exact package price from your airport to each destination, call American Airlines. Just as an example, however, here are a few of the possible add-ons from certain cities in the country:

Chicago to Acapulco	Add on $110 per person
Houston to Mexico City	Add on $20 per person
Oklahoma City to Cancun	Add on $47 per person
New Orleans to Puerto Vallarta	Add on $62 per person

As you can see, the add-ons aren't that big a deal, but must be taken into consideration when estimating your total trip expense. Call American Airlines Fly A'Away Vacations at (800)321-2121.

- DELTA DREAM VACATIONS
    Acapulco—Packages start at $445 per person
    Puerto Vallarta—Packages start at $487 per person
    Cancun—Packages start at $570 per person
    Cozumel—Packages start at $611 per person
  All these package deals include four-days and three-nights accommodations, round-trip airfare via Delta Air Lines, round-trip airport transfers and various taxes. The prices quoted above are for trips originating in San Francisco; call Delta directly to find out what they cost from your airport.

This is by no means an all-inclusive list of package deals to Mexico; and the prices will obviously be higher or lower by the time you read this book. This should whet your appetite, however, when you see how affordable it is to honeymoon in Mexico.

CRUISING

There is another way to get there—how about cruising to Mexico? After interviewing many couples who spent their honeymoons in Mexico, I found that those who took a cruise really loved it. For one thing, all your stuff is in your cabin on the ship, so when you dock at the various Mexican ports for a day or two, you always have your very own room to return to each evening. Also, since meals are served on board, the only meals you will eat in Mexico probably will be your lunches, saving money on your food budget. Some cruises even offer to prepare a picnic for you to take to the beach or on a hike, something many couples enjoy. If you want to indulge in a tasty Mexican meal while in Mexico, however, you certainly can.

When you cruise to Mexico, you will probably depart from Los Angeles or San Diego, which means that you will need to pay the add-on airfare from your part of the country to the port of departure. Many of the cruise lines' fares include airfare, so you will need to ask.

If you have never taken a cruise before, it is an experience in itself. Never will you be so pampered again in your life; several people cater to you at one time, offering you everything from towels by the pool to enticing buffet meals every couple of hours, to superb entertainment. It is typical to gain a pound a day while on a cruise, because it's impossible to resist the piles of delicious food. In any case, a cruise not only affords you the hot beach honeymoon that Mexico offers, but is an exciting and memorable experience in itself.

On the next few pages, we'll look at some of the cruises available to Mexico.

- COMMODORE CRUISE LINE
  This cruise line offers a six-night, seven-day cruise from San Diego to the Mexican Riviera, including Cabo San Lucas, Mazatlan and Puerto Vallarta. They offer a rate of $473 per person that does not include port charges or taxes. Their cruises can be

arranged through Cruise Holidays at (800)877-9876, and probably through a travel agency in your hometown.

- NORWEGIAN CRUISE LINE
  Norwegian has a special rate for honeymooning couples, offering one-half off their regular rate for the spouse. (They require that you fill out an affidavit regarding your wedding date, etc.) A four-day cruise from Los Angeles to Catalina Island, San Diego and Ensenada, Mexico, starts at about $900 per couple (including the one-half off honey-mooner deal). They also have a three-day cruise departing from Los Angeles that starts at about $750 per couple. They provide add-on rates for airfare to Los Angeles from your home airport. Check with your travel agent for Norwegian Cruise Line's latest brochure, which includes all prices, including add-on airfares.

- OTHER CRUISE OPTIONS
  Be sure to watch the travel sections of the big-city Sunday newspapers near your home-town; this is where many of the great cruise deals are advertised, and the prices will usually include any add-on airfare from your state.

  Listed below are some other discount cruise companies that can save you money off the cruise lines' brochure rates.
  —World Wide Cruises (800)882-9000
  in Florida: (305)720-9000
  —Cruises of Distinction (800)634-3445
  —Landry & Kling (800)431-4007
  —The Cruise Line, Inc. (800)777-0707
  —Cruise Collection, Inc. (800)444-9060
  —The Travel Company (800)367-6090
  Call each one and ask for a brochure, then compare each cruise line's price with discount company rates. You will find many different prices for the exact same cruise on the exact same day in the exact same cabin, so take the time to shop around; it will definitely save you money.

A La Carte Planning

If you want to plan the trip yourself, avoiding the package or cruise tours, you will need to price all the components—airfares, accommodations, meals, car rentals, tips, etc. Here are some price guidelines for each of these components.

AIRLINE FARES

- MEXICANA AIRLINES (800)531-7921

  Here is an example of one of their round-trip fares:

Phoenix-Cabo San Lucas	$289 per person

- ALASKA AIRLINES (800)426-0333

  Here are a couple of their typical round-trip fares:

San Francisco-Mazatlan	$341 per person
San Francisco-Puerto Vallarta	$386 per person

- SUNTRIPS (415)394-7700

  They currently offer these round-trip fares, from California to these various destinations:

Mazatlan	$149 per person
Puerto Vallarta	$169 per person
Cabo San Lucas	$169 per person
Cancun	$269 per person

Also, be sure to use the cost-cutting airfare ideas from chapter 3 when making your reservations.

ACCOMMODATIONS

- FIESTA AMERICANA MEXICO

  This tour company is operated by Fiesta Americana Hotels, a division of Posadas de Mexico. Their packages include a stay at one of their hotels, where they especially cater to honeymooners by offering special, romantic extra touches. Just a few of their offerings follow; you will need to call them for a brochure that will give you all the current package prices from your part of the country. These prices do not include airfare.

  ### Cancun

  Fiesta Americana Cancun

  Four days, three nights, plus welcome cocktail, flowers, daily breakfast, one Mexican dinner, and room tax. Cost: $448 per couple.

  Hyatt Cancun Caribe

  Five days, four nights, plus daily breakfast, champagne, flowers, one dinner at Blue Bayou, and airport limo. Cost: $760 per couple.

  ### Puerto Vallarta

  Hotel Buenaventura

  Four days, three nights, plus daily breakfast, bottle of champagne, one dinner for two, a welcome drink, and tax. Cost: $282 per couple.

Hotel Quinta Real Villas & Golf

Seven days, six nights, plus daily breakfast, champagne, and no cover charge in disco. Cost: $865 per couple.

Acapulco

Fiesta Americana Condesa Acapulco

Four days, three nights, plus champagne, flowers, buffet breakfast, one dinner with wine, and bathrobes. Cost: $501 per couple.

Call Fiesta Americana Mexico at (800)969-3222.

- CONTACT THE HOTEL DIRECTLY

You can also make your reservations directly with the hotels of your choice. Here is a list of reasonably priced hotels, rated at least three-star or better, all located close to the beach, if not right on it.

Acapulco

Acapulco Plaza Holiday Inn

Two swimming pools, beach access, rental boats, sauna, whirlpool, waterskiing, scuba diving, lighted tennis courts, parachute rides. Phone: 01152(748)5-90-50. Cost: $50 to $70 per night.

Las Hamacas Hotel

All rooms have a balcony; amenities include a swimming pool, rental boats, beach pavilion, private pier, fishing and waterskiing. Phone: 01152(748)3-77-46. Cost: $50 to $70 per night.

Cabo San Lucas

Hotel Clarion Cabo San Lucas

On a bluff overlooking the ocean; offers three swimming pools, beach access, whirl-pools, charter fishing and snorkeling. Phone: 01152(684)3-0044. Cost: $70 to $100 per night.

Hotel Plaza Las Glorias

Located on the marina; offers cable TV, movies, swimming pool, charter fishing, water taxi to beach club. Phone: 01152(684)3-1220. Cost: About $75 per night.

Cancun

Holiday Inn Crowne Plaza

On the beach; offers cable TV, movies, three swimming pools, sauna, whirlpool and lighted tennis courts. Phone: 01152(988)5-10-50. Cost: $100 to $140 per night.

Radisson Paraiso Cancun

Located on the beach; all rooms have an ocean view and cable TV, plus you'll enjoy fishing, waterskiing and lighted tennis courts. Phone: 01152(988)5-0108. Cost: $85 to $125 per night.

Ensenada

Las Rosas Hotel and Spa

On a bluff overlooking the ocean; ask for a room with a balcony, ocean view and fireplace. You'll also find cable TV, movies, a heated pool, sauna, whirlpool, racquetball, and a masseuse. Phone: 01152(667)4-4320. Cost: About $85 per night.

Puerto Vallarta

Holiday Inn

You'll find two swimming pools, a beach, whirlpools, rental boats, fishing, lighted tennis courts, waterskiing, windsurfing, scuba equipment and parachute rides awaiting when you arrive. Phone: 01152(322)2-17-00. Cost: $70 to $100 per night.

Hotel Plaza Las Glorias

Offers a beach, rental boats, cable TV and movies. Phone: 01152(322)2-22-24. Cost: $80 to $100 per night.

DINING

Acapulco

Dino's, Costera M Aleman 137

Open-air terrace dining with a bay view. Great Italian food. Cost: About $20 for two.

Restaurant El Jardin (in the Las Hamacas Hotel)

Specializes in seafood and Mexican dishes. Cost: $30 for two.

Cabo San Lucas

Melia San Lucas Hotel Restaurant

Offers enjoyable, affordable Mexican meals. Cost: About $15 for two.

Coconuts Restaurant, located in the Club Cascadas de Baja

Offers seafood specialties in a tropical beach setting. Cost: About $30 for two.

Cancun

Stouffer Presidente-Cancun Restaurant

Serves many excellent Mexican dishes; there is entertainment as well. Cost: About $24 for two.

Ensenada

Las Rosas Hotel and Spa on Highway 1

Has great Mexican food starting at only $5 per person. Cost: About $12 for two.

Puerto Vallarta

Hyatt Coral Grand Hotel

Another four-star hotel with a reasonably priced restaurant. Their entrees start at only $6 per person. Cost: About $14 for two.

CAR RENTALS

Because taxis are so affordable and available, you will only need a rental car for the side trips. Many of these trips are along rough roads, so you will probably want to rent a jeep, which must be reserved in advance. Car rentals are more expensive in Mexico than in the U.S. Just as an example, Hertz offers an economy car in Puerto Vallarta at the rate of $230 per week or $40 per day, plus a 10 percent Mexican tax. You may not need a car for more than a day or two because most of your activities will be easily accessible within the city itself. Many of the car rental companies recommend that you reserve your rental at least three days in advance, preferably before you leave the United States.

FREE OR LOW-COST ATTRACTIONS

Mexico is an adult playground, with water sports, shopping, and dozens of other affordable activities. There is sport fishing, boating, waterskiing, scuba diving, swimming, wind surfing and snorkeling; or you can take a parasail ride, rent a bicycle, take a hike, or just hang out at the hotel with its pools, sauna, tennis courts and hot sand beach. In addition to all these "givens," each Mexican city is known for some special attractions. Here are a few:

Acapulco
- Shop for bargains. Popular purchases are leather goods, pottery, silver, and glassware blown by artisans.
- Watch the diving from LaQuebrada Cliff.
- If you're in Acapulco on a Sunday, you may want to attend a bullfight. Buy tickets near the top of the arena because they are less expensive and give a sweeping view of the spectacle.
- Take a calandrias (horse-drawn carriage) on a tour of the city.

Cabo San Lucas
- Take a one-hour skiff ride around the tip of the peninsula.
- Shop at the many craft shops in the center of town where artisans display their distinctive, black coral jewelry.

Cancun
- One of the most popular activities in the Cancun area is viewing the Mayan ruins, some of which can be seen on various sightseeing tours; others can be viewed by taking an inexpensive cab ride to the Pok-Ta-Pok site on the Robert Trent Jones Golf Course. You can also view Mayan temples on the grounds of the Camino Real and Cancun Sheraton Hotels.

Ensenada
- Rent a jeep and take Highway 1 to the eighteenth-century ruins of two missions built by Dominican friars.
- Take a tour of the Bodegas de Santo Tomas winery, Mexico's largest.

Puerto Vallarta
- Rent a horse by the hour (available at several of the larger hotels), and ride along the

trails that surround the city and follow the shore.

- Enjoy Puerto Vallarta's nightlife. It is a real partying town with plenty of lively entertainment into the wee morning hours.
- Shop at the famous boutiques along Avenida Juarez.

Special Splurges

Acapulco
- Have dinner at Le Gourmet Restaurant in the Acapulco Princess Hotel, complete with entertainment. Cost: About $70 for two.

Cabo San Lucas
- Enjoy a six-course Mexican dinner at Villa Alfonso's Restaurant. Cost: About $80 for two.

Cancun
- Try dinner at Calypso's, on the beach at Punta Cancun. There is a Caribbean ambience and plenty of entertainment. Cost: About $50 for two.

Ensenada
- El Rey Sol Restaurant on Ave Blancarte is the place to go for Mexican food. Cost: About $40 for two.

Puerto Vallarta
- Try La Peria at Carretera Mex 200 in Camino Real. This is one of the nicest restaurants in town; you will definitely need reservations. Cost: About $50 for two.

Helpful Hints for Traveling to Mexico

- Contact the Mexican Government Tourist Office, 405 Park Avenue, Suite 1002, New York, NY 10022, or call them at (800)262-8900. They will send lots of interesting and helpful tourist information to help you select your destination.
- If you plan to drive a car into Mexico, you will need Mexican insurance; your American car insurance won't be worth a thing in Mexico. Go to your insurance company and purchase a special policy that adheres to Mexican law. Here is an example of the cost of an insurance policy, good for seven days, for a car valued at $8,000:

Collision	$1.95 per day
Fire & Theft	.98 per day
Property Damage	.47 per day
Bodily Injury	2.24 per day
Medical	.38 per day

Including an expense fee, the total cost is $45.14.

- If you will be traveling more than 12 miles into Mexico, you will also be required to carry these documents:
  1. Vehicle title (original only) *or* a notarized affidavit of consent from the legal owner (if you're not the legal owner) *or* a rental agreement and a notarized affidavit of consent from the rental company. If you are making payments to a bank, and the bank is the legal owner of your car, you will need a notarized affidavit of consent from that lender.
  2. A receipt for a nonrefundable $10 fee which you must pay as you enter the country if you plan to travel more than 12 miles into Mexico. This must be charged on a major credit card (no checks or cash accepted).
  3. Instead of the receipt, you may carry a surety bond issued by a Mexican company for the entire blue book value of the vehicle. The bond must be purchased at the border and is refundable only at the point of purchase when the vehicle leaves Mexico. (You *must* enter and depart Mexico at the exact same border point.)
- In addition to all of the above, you will also need to carry with you:
  1. Proof of nationality (birth certificate or passport). A driver's license is *not* considered proof of nationality.
  2. A tourist card.
  3. Driver's license.
- It is a good idea to carry U.S. traveler's checks into Mexico, preferably in small denominations; cash them as they are needed.
- Don't drink the water in Mexico; instead, drink canned or bottled carbonated beverages or beverages made with boiled water, such as coffee or tea. Many hotels provide bottled water for their guests. Don't even use tap water for brushing your teeth or cleaning your contact lenses; use chemical disinfecting tablets to purify water used for these purposes. You can purchase these tablets in the United States or at pharmacies or supermarkets in Mexico.
- It is wise to make a visit to your own personal physician before taking your trip; ask about the health precautions you can take while in Mexico.

If you choose Mexico for your honeymoon, you will have an exciting, colorful time, and you'll be able to afford it, which is the best part!

CHAPTER 23

OUT OF THIS WORLD
Affordable Alaskan Honeymoons

For most people, the biggest expense of an Alaskan honeymoon will be transportation. Of course, that's something honeymooning residents of Alaska don't need to worry about — and that means more money available for activities and luxuries when they begin to budget for their trip. For the rest of us, just *getting there* is a major consideration.

It would be nice if you could cruise to Alaska, but, unfortunately, that puts us over a total honeymoon budget of $1,500. Most Alaskan cruises start at about $850 per person, plus add-on airfare to the point of departure, plus tips, plus spending money. You can drive to Alaska on the Alaskan Highway, but that is a time-consuming trip, averaging seven days of driving each way from Seattle to Fairbanks. If you have the time, and it sounds like fun, then go for it. The highway is open year-round, so that is at least a possibility.

The third, and most likely, alternative for those of us who have to *get* to Alaska before we can enjoy Alaska is to fly. At the time of this book's publication the average round-trip fare from many mainland cities to Alaska was about $550 per person. If you are very careful with your spending once you're in Alaska, you can still stay within the $1,500 limit. In the following pages you'll find a couple of Alaskan destinations that may work for you.

HONEYMOON NO. 1 — ANCHORAGE — DENALI NATIONAL PARK

Route
- Highway 3 north out of Anchorage to Denali National Park.

Romantic Appeal
- Nature lovers are pleasantly surprised by Anchorage's mild climate, which allows hours of outdoor, honeymoon fun.

Free Attractions
- Take a walking tour of Anchorage. Maps are available at the Log Cabin Visitor Information center at Fourth Avenue and F Street.
- Enjoy one of Anchorage's two yearly festivals: The 10-day Fur Rendezvous in early February or the Iditarod Trail Race in early March.
- Chugach State Park surrounds Anchorage on three sides and affords many free activi-

ties, including guided nature walks, berry picking, wildlife watching, or cross-country skiing in the winter.

- Take a guided tour of Fort Richardson Wildlife Center, 9 miles north of downtown Anchorage on Glenn Highway.
- Explore Kantishna, a semi-abandoned mining town on the eastern boundary of Denali National Park.
- Enjoy a drive along the George Parks Highway (Highway 3) that runs along the eastern border of the Denali National park and offers sweeping views of the alpine scenery. (Bring your camera.)
- Watch a sled dog demonstration at the Denali Park's kennels; they are conducted three times daily during the summer.

Low-Cost Attractions
- Alaska Aviation Heritage Museum, 4721 Aircraft Drive, Anchorage. Cost: $5.
- Alaska Experience Theater, 705 West Sixth Avenue, presents "Alaska the Greatland." Cost: $6.
- Alaska Zoo, on O'Malley Road in Anchorage. Cost: $5.
- Anchorage Museum of History and Art, 121 West Seventh Avenue. Cost: $3.
- The Imaginarium, Fifth Avenue and G Street, Anchorage. This is a nature and science "discovery center" with a re-created polar bear den, etc. Cost: $4.
- Visit the Oscar Anderson House, 420 M Street, Anchorage, built by a Swedish immigrant in 1915. Cost: $2.

Special Splurges
- Take a whitewater rafting trip down the Matanusaka River. The trips are conducted by Nova Riverunners of Alaska and depart from Kings Mountain Lodge on Glenn Highway in Anchorage. Cost: $40 to $60 per person.
- Enjoy a five-and-a-half-hour cruise of Prince William Sound, including the College and Harriman Fjords. Reservations are made through 26 Glacier Cruise, 509 West Fourth Avenue, Anchorage. Cost: $119 per person.
- Enjoy dinner at the Crow's Nest Restaurant on the twentieth floor of The Hotel Captain Cook in Anchorage. You'll have a rooftop panoramic view of the city, mountain and Cook Inlet. Cost: About $75 for two.
- Take a Tundra Wildlife Tour to Toklat River. Driver-guides explain the geology, flora and fauna on the six-hour trip. These tours depart from Denali Park Station Hotel daily at 6 A.M. and 3 P.M. Cost: $41 per person (includes a box lunch).
- Owl Rafting in Denali Park off Parks Highway, milepost 238, offers two-hour trips through the Nenana River Canyon. Cost: $36 per person.
- Denali Raft Adventures offers guided whitewater raft trips of the Nenana River with

views of Alaskan scenery and wildlife. There are day and evening runs that last from two to six hours. Cost: two-hour trip, $34 per person; four-hour trip, $54 per person; six-hour trip, $125 per person.

Honeymoon No. 2 — Fairbanks — Denali National Park

Route
- Highway 3 south out of Fairbanks to Denali National Park.

Romantic Appeal
- Historical Fairbanks provides honeymooners with a home base for all their romantic side trips.

Free Attractions
- Walking tour of Fairbanks; pick up brochures and a map at the Log Cabin Visitor Information Center, 550 First Avenue, Fairbanks.
- Cripple Creek Resort, in Ester, 8 miles west on Highway 3, includes buildings that date back to 1904. Transportation is available from many of the local hotels.
- National Oceanic Atmospheric Tracking Station on Steese Highway offers free guided tours.
- Enjoy the free attractions in Denali National Park as explained under Alaskan Honeymoon No. 1.

Low-Cost Attractions
- Enjoy "Photosymphony" at the Firehouse Theater. Cost: $5.
- A one-hour performance that recounts the gold rush days is called "Service With a Smile" and is presented in the Malemute Saloon. Cost: $8.
- On Goldstream Road, tour the *Gold Dredge Numer 8* which is a five-deck ship built in 1928 to ply Goldstream and Engineer creeks for gold. Cost: $8.

Special Splurges
- Take a four-hour trip on the *Discovery III*, a sternwheeler docked off Airport Way on Discovery Road in Fairbanks. The trip includes a stop at an Indian village and a dogsled demonstration. Cost: $29.50 per person.
- Enjoy a very special honeymoon dinner at the Bear and Seal Restaurant in the Westmark Fairbanks Hotel. It is advertised as a "refined, intimate atmosphere." Cost: About $75 for two.
- Enjoy the special splurges available in Denali National Park, explained under Alaskan Honeymoon No. 1.

CHAPTER 24
THE CARIBBEAN CALLS
Affordable Island Honeymoons

They say God created the Caribbean for honeymooners. It could be true when you consider the unashamedly romantic setting, with the warmth of its sea breezes, its intimate coves, white sand beaches, flowered gardens and tropical luxury. Add to this the hundreds of things to do and see, and there won't be enough hours in the day to experience it all!

The trick is to have all this romance on less than $1,500. It's not as difficult as you may think. One way is to fly to a destination that has affordable lodging and meals. This can be accomplished by planning the trip yourself or purchasing a package plan that includes airfare. The second way is to take a three- or four-day cruise (the longer cruises are too expensive). Obviously, a Caribbean cruise will be more affordable for those of you who live closer to the East Coast.

Let's look at a sample of package deals.

PACKAGE DEALS

These packages are offered through travel agencies, airlines, and independent tour companies that specialize in Caribbean vacations. They are a little difficult to compare because some include airfare and hotel, while others also include some or all of these extras: meals, beverages, entertainment, round-trip airport transfers, welcome parties, taxes, tips, service charges, a rental car, free use of all sports equipment, tennis, golf, bicycling, horseback riding, 24-hour complimentary room service, free valet, manicures, pedicures, dry cleaning, paddle boating, fitness center, pool tables, use of motor scooters, and "anytime snacks."

When any or all of these goodies are in one package deal, it is usually called an All-Inclusive plan; when the package mainly consists of airfare and hotel accommodations, it is usually called a Hotel Package. Here are a few of the companies offering package plans to the Caribbean:

- FLING VACATIONS
  This company specializes in air/hotel packages. A typical deal is their Nassau Fling that includes airfare and hotel for three nights at $329 per person. This rate is based on their lowest midweek departure from a Zone 1 city, such as Philadelphia. It does not include taxes and security fees. Call them at (800)523-9624, or ask a travel agent for an up-to-date Fling Vacations catalog.

- SUPERCLUBS

This company has a variety of plans including Hotel Packages and All-Inclusive Vacations. The information in their catalog would fill a couple of my chapters, but here is an enticing sampling of what they offer:

Typical Hotel Package: Seven days and six nights, including airfare, airport transfers, all hotel taxes and service charges at $349 per person for an ocean view room at the Golden Seas Resort in Ochos Rios, Jamaica.

Typical All-Inclusive Vacation: Four days and three nights, including airfare, all meals, beverages, tennis, water sports, entertainment, airport transfers, welcome party, taxes, tips and service charge at $789 per person for a "superior" room at Club Jamaica at Eaton Hall. This resort is right on the ocean, and is considered an "intimate hide-a-way for all the fun of tropical romance."

Their airfares, when included in their packages, are based on midweek travel from Miami. You will need to add on round-trip airfare from your departure city. Here are a few of their add-on airfares to Miami:
— From Atlanta $180 per person
— From Detroit $180 per person
— From San Francisco $330 per person
— From Chicago $220 per person
SuperClubs also offers desirable all-inclusive honeymoons at couples-only resorts, a concept that may be appealing to you, although a little more expensive. Ask about them when you call for a free catalog at (800)858-8009 or (516)868-6924.

- AMERICAN AIRLINES FLY A'AWAY VACATIONS

You can book a Hotel Package or All-Inclusive Vacation through American Airlines, but their prices do not include airfare. Here are a couple of their offerings:

Anguilla. A four-day, three-night stay at Mariners Hotel, including all meals and beverages, windsurfing, sailing, games, airport transfers, hotel taxes, service charges and surcharges, all at a cost of $468 per person. Add to this your airfare and spending money. An extra night's stay will cost about $150 more per person.

St. Martin. The same number of days and nights at the Flamboyant Bounty I Hotel, including all meals and beverages, snorkeling, windsurfing, games, airport transfers, hotel taxes, service charges and surcharges, has a cost of $375 per person. Of course, add on your airfare and spending money. A four-night stay is about $125 more per person.

American Airlines also has hotel packages that do not include meals or beverages. American Airlines Fly A'Away Vacations has a free 36-page catalog that details various plans and destinations, including Anguilla, Antigua, Aruba, The Bahamas, Barbados, Bermuda, Cayman Islands, Dominican Republic, The Family Islands, Grenada, Guadeloupe, Jamaica, Martinique, Puerto Rico, St. Croix, St. John, St. Kitts, Nevis, St. Lucia, St. Martin, St. Thomas, Tortola, Virgin Gorda and Trinidad. Call them at (800)833-5767.

These are only a few of the companies offering various packages to the Caribbean. Drop by a travel agency to pick up an armful of brochures from all the companies offering package deals for Caribbean vacations.

CRUISING

Here is my favorite way to vacation in the Caribbean; I like the idea of having my own bed each night and visiting ports along the way. Cruising is such an easy way to travel because everything is planned for you and, best of all, most of your expenses are included in one tab. The few added expenses that you will have can be calculated in advance, so there won't be surprises. You will need money for tips, on-board gift purchases, certain alcoholic beverages, specialty services, etc. All your food, lodging and on-board entertainment is included in the base price. Most cruise lines will discount the fare up to 15 percent for advance booking.

There are several cruises available, and as I mentioned at the beginning of this chapter, if you want to hold your total honeymoon expense under $1,500, you will probably want to go on a 3- or 4-night trip. If you can afford to spend a little more, you can take a five-, six- or seven-night cruise. Let's look at some of the most popular Caribbean cruises in the under $1,500 category.

- ROYAL CARIBBEAN
  This cruise line specializes in three- and four-night cruises to the Bahamas. Their fares include the cruise itself and usually round-trip airfare from their gateway cities. If you're not flying from a gateway city, there may be an add-on fee depending on your city and *booking category*. The booking category depends on which deck you select for your cabin location and whether you are sailing in Peak Season, Value Season, or Economy Seson. You'll need to give them a call to determine the fare for your honeymoon dates and your departure city. Generally, however, you can take a three-night cruise starting at about $465 per person in Economy Season, or a four-night cruise starting at about $585. Depending on whether you have add-on airfare or not, these reasonable fares will obviously leave you with money to spend on some of the port activities. Call (800)327-6700 or, in Florida, (800)432-6559.

- PREMIER'S BIG RED BOAT
  This is the official cruise line of Walt Disney World. Their three- or four-night cruises to the Bahamas include visits to Disney World and Epcot Center, plus several other attractions. Prices start at $445 per person for a three-day cruise and $575 for a four-day cruise. They specialize in Honeymoons-at-Sea, which include chilled champagne in your cabin, a special cocktail party, etc. Contact your travel agent or call (800)473-3262. They even have a videotape you can order that will give you a preview of the cruise.

- CARNIVAL
  This cruise line also caters to honeymooners, who sail from Miami to the Caribbean on the *Ecstasy*. Their three-day cruises start at about $459 per person; four-day cruises start at about $579. Prices include round-trip airfare from over 150 cities, with an add-on cost for "Category 3 cities and cities west of the Rockies." Their special Honeymoon Fun Ship inclusions are a complimentary honeymoon champagne party, complimentary souvenir photos, and a spacious honeymoon stateroom with queen- or king-size bed. Call Carnival at (800)327-7373 for exact fare from your home city, or call their Honeymoon Hotline at (800)727-2717.

- NORWEGIAN CRUISE LINE
  Norwegian offers three- and four-day cruises to the Caribbean with stops at two or three ports. Their fares start at about $575 per person for a three-day cruise and $635 for four days. Airfare may be included, depending on your city of departure; however, reasonably priced add-on airfares are available. Like most cruise lines, they love honeymooners. Call them at (800)262-4NCL.

These are only a few of the Caribbean cruises available, and while any travel agent can book a cruise, many travel experts advise honeymooners to book through a "cruise-only" agent, which may be your best source of information on each ship's personality. Also, a cruise-only agency will have access to the best cabins at the lowest possible prices. A list of cruise-only agencies is provided in the Resources section of this book. I have seen some of these agency's brochures. With the savings they offer, you may be able to book up to seven days instead of just three or four.

The key is this: Shop around. Prices vary for the same cruise. Search for the best price.

A La Carte Planning

You may be able to design your Caribbean honeymoon for even less than package prices by arranging your own airfare and accommodations. Use the ideas in chapter 3 to get the best airfare possible; then use a AAA *Travel Guide* or *Mobile Tour Book* to find your accommodations.

AIRLINE FARES

Here are some sample round-trip airfares to Miami from various cities.

From San Francisco $500
From Phoenix $420
From Seattle $500
From San Diego $470
From Chicago $380
From Nashville $440
From Pittsburgh $400

This is in addition to the airfare from Miami to your Caribbean destination. You will notice that these fares are considerably higher than the add-on airfares charged in conjunction with a Hotel Package or All-Inclusive Vacation.

ACCOMMODATIONS

Here are hotel suggestions for some of the more popular Caribbean destinations.

- ANTIGUA, WEST INDIES
  Copper & Lumber Store Hotel, English Harbour. This is an historic country inn with a nautical atmosphere. Call (809)460-1058. Cost: About $100 to $175 per night.
- ARUBA
  Aruba Palm Beach Resort and Casino, Oranjestad, located on the beach. This resort includes lighted tennis courts. Call (297)8-23900. Cost: About $90 to $160 per night.
- BAHAMAS
  Romora Bay Club on Harbour Island offers hillside cottages overlooking the harbor. Call (809)333-2324. Cost: About $85 to $115 per night.
- BARBADOS
  Barbados Beach Village, Bridgetown, is located on the beach with tennis and water sports available. Call (809)425-1440. Cost: About $90 to $150 per night.
- BERMUDA
  Princess Hotel, Hamilton, Pembroke Parish, sits on the edge of Hamilton Harbour with water tours and massage available. Call (809)295-3000. Cost: $120 to $170 per night.
- CAYMAN ISLANDS
  Brac Reef Beach Resort, Cayman Brac, is located on the beachfront with tennis and bicycles available. Call (809)948-7323. Cost: About $79 to $110 per night.
- JAMAICA
  Oceana Hotel, Kingston, overlooks Kingston Harbor. Call (809)922-0920. Cost: About $90 per night.

- PUERTO RICO
  Best Western Hotel Pierre, San Juan, includes a very nice pool courtyard. Call (809)721-1200. Cost: About $99 to $117 per night.
- VIRGIN ISLANDS, U.S.
  Hotel 1829, St. Thomas, is a historic country inn overlooking the bay. Call (809)776-1829. Cost: About $70 per night.

DINING

Now, here are a few of the more affordable dining ideas.

- ANTIGUA, WEST INDIES
  You can eat fairly reasonably at the previously recommended Copper & Lumber Store Hotel. Cost: Dinner for two, about $30.
- ARUBA
  Divide your meals between three hotel restaurants: Talk of the Town Resort Hotel, Bucuti Beach Resort and Manchebo Beach Resort. You can enjoy a nice meal at any of these spots. Cost: About $20 for two.
- BAHAMAS
  Try the buffet lunch at the Romora Bay Club. Cost: About $25 for two.
- BARBADOS
  The Barbados Hilton terrace dining room and the Marriott-Sam Lord's Castle restaurant offer great meals. Cost: About $20 for two.
- BERMUDA
  The Princess Hotel in Hamilton has a couple of very nice restaurants where you can enjoy a meal. Cost: About $30 for two.
- CAYMAN ISLANDS
  The Brac Reef Beach Resort serves excellent dinners. Cost: About $40 for two.
- JAMAICA
  All of the major hotels in Kingston serve affordable meals. Give them a try. Cost: Entrees start at $10 to $12 per person.
- PUERTO RICO
  There is a stylish cafe-bistro in old San Juan at San Sebastian 106 that serves Puerto Rican cuisine, local produce is a specialty. Cost: About $30 for two.
- VIRGIN ISLANDS, U.S.
  Both of the Bolongos—the Bolongo at Elysian Beach and the Bolongo Bay Beach and Tennis Club—have fun eats. Cost: About $20 for two.

CAR RENTALS

When it comes to car rentals, most tourists take advantage of the reasonable taxi fares instead, due to the difficult driving conditions on the islands. Some Caribbean countries, such as Bermuda, do not allow a nonresident to drive a car; in fact, rental cars are not available. Tourists who need a car for the day can hire an all-day taxi which comes complete with a driver. Other popular modes of transportation are scooters and bicycles, both easily accessible. Ferries are also affordable and practical, and a ferry ride can be a lot of fun.

Those of you who do decide to rent a car where allowed should make the reservation beforehand; it will cost between $25 and $50 per day.

FREE OR LOW-COST ATTRACTIONS

If you decide to cruise the Caribbean, there will be so many activities planned you will welcome some private time in your cabin. Nothing beats all the pampering you receive while on a cruise, plus all your decisions are made for you—when to eat, what to eat, where to sleep, where to play. Even when your ship docks at the various ports you will be given a suggested itinerary, plus a picnic lunch if you like. Cruising is the lazy life—a much deserved rest after all the busy wedding plans.

If you're going to spend your time on land, however, that's another story. You will need to make plans to fill each day with a few of the hundreds of activities available. The Caribbean is known for its water sports, of course. It's especially famous for its clear water that affords divers and snorkelers wonderful afternoons in the warm ocean waters.

In addition to all the water sports, there are many historical places to see and much other fun stuff to do. Whether you plan your own itinerary or take a package air/hotel tour, you will be provided with dozens of brochures explaining all the local attractions. Here are a few to choose from at the more popular Caribbean destinations:

- ANTIGUA, WEST INDIES
  Known for its luxury yachts, Antigua offers people-watching down at the yacht harbor. Enjoy Carnival Week if you're there the last week of July, and if you're not, enjoy the nightlife at the many small nightclubs and five casinos.
- ARUBA
  Many hotel casinos and nightclubs offer evening entertainment, including folkloric, limbo and steel band shows. Enjoy Aruba's Mardi Gras if you happen to be there in February, or the annual Aruba Jazz and Latin Music Festival in June.
- BAHAMAS
  The Bahamas are a string of islands, each with its own special attraction. Freeport Islands is a resort in itself, offering shows with top-name entertainers. Harbour Island boasts one of the oldest settlements in the Bahamas, Dunmore Town, a fun spot for a walking tour. Nassau is the capital city of the Bahamas, located on New Providence Island. It is loaded with attractions, including three eighteenth-century forts, horse-

drawn carriage rides, and a great zoo and botanical garden. Paradise Island has one of the finest beaches in the Bahamas, plus a "strip" that includes a casino and theater.

- BARBADOS
Barbados is famous for its eastern coast swimming beaches, plus the Folkestone Underwater Park, the Marine Museum, and lively nightlife featuring the limbo and calypso.

- BERMUDA
Called the showcase of the British Commonwealth, the town of Hamilton is known for its shops, which feature antiques, woolens, silver, English china, French perfumes and German cameras. Hamilton Parish is also famous for its Crystal Caves, accessible by climbing 81 steps. St. George's, on St. George's Island, is a storybook town with narrow, twisting lanes. In St. George's, you can visit the Carriage Museum, Carter House, Historical Society Museum and Tucker House. If you're vacationing in Bermuda, don't miss two attractions at Smith's Parish: the Bermuda Aquarium and Zoo and Devil's Hole, an aquarium harboring shark and sea turtles in a natural setting.

- CAYMAN ISLANDS
Grand Cayman is famous for its driving tour, running south from George Town along the South Sound coastal road. George Town itself boasts of its national museum, Maritime and Treasure Museum, and its Turtle Farm.

- JAMAICA
Jamaica is known for its free-port shops in Kingston, Montego Bay, Port Antonio and Ochos Rios. Items sold in these shops are free of customs duties, so "shop 'til you drop." In addition to shopping, you will enjoy the fabulous floorshows presented at the larger nightclubs and cabarets. There are also plantation tours, botanical gardens, river rafting, and many museums and historical sites.

- PUERTO RICO
A "must-see" while in old San Juan is Calle Fortaleza where you can shop for traditional island crafts and watch local artisans doing their thing. Some of the most notable crafts are lace, hand-carved religious figures, linens, copper, gold and silver filigree jewelry, scarves, hammocks, baskets and musical instruments. Old San Juan has become known as an international art center because of the quality of its wares. Also, you can take various driving tours that include El Morro Castle, Fort San Cristobal, San Jose Church and Cristo Chapel. You will also want to visit the Plaza De San Jose, La Casa De Callejeon and Casa Blanco, a fortified white mansion erected in 1523 for Ponce de Leon.

- VIRGIN ISLANDS, U.S.
On the island of St. Croix, you'll want to go horseback riding on some of the magnificent trails, or take a glass-bottom boat or catamaran trip to Buck Island. In Charlotte Amalie you can visit Coral World, an underwater observatory in a three-story tower standing 100 feet offshore.

SPECIAL SPLURGES

- ARUBA

  Take a ride on the Atlantis Submarine, departing from the Seaport Village Marina in Oranjestad. Cost: $68.

- BAHAMAS

  If you're in Nassau, you must take Hartley's Undersea Walk, departing from the Nassau Yacht Haven. It's a three-and-a-half-hour excursion that gives you the chance to walk on the sea floor. Cost: $35.

- BERMUDA

  In Sandys Parish the submarine *Enterprise* departs from the dock at the Royal Naval Dockyard on Ireland Island. It affords a 45-minute underwater look at a 1878 shipwreck and coral formations. Cost: $60.

- CAYMAN ISLANDS

  Rent a 16-foot motorboat for a half day. The boat includes a safety package with VHF radio. The rental company is called Pleasure Boat Rentals and is located at the Grand Pavilion Hotel in Grand Cayman. Cost: $99.

- JAMAICA

  In Montego Bay there is a canoe ride called "An Evening on the Great River" that takes you up the torch-lit river to a village where there is a native floor show of music and dancing. The canoe departs 10 miles west of Montego Bay off Route A1. It's best to take a shuttle from one of the hotels. Cost: $50.

- PUERTO RICO

  Take an Island Mariner Cruise on a voyage around the San Juans. The seven-hour cruise departs from Bellingham and covers about 90 miles. You must make reservations by calling (206)734-8866. Cost: $40.

- Available on many of the Caribbean Islands: Glass-bottom boat rides, deep-sea diving lessons, horseback riding, ferry rides, mini-cruises, championship golf, fabulous night-club entertainment, elegant dining with seafood specialties, parasailing, deep-sea fishing excursions, with guides, and helicopter tours.

HELPFUL HINTS FOR TRAVELING IN THE CARIBBEAN

- As soon as you arrive at your destination, head for the visitors' information center for brochures, maps, and tips on the island's customs, attractions, driving tours, currency and type of electricity. (If you try to plug your U.S. hair dryer into a 210-230 volt plug, you will burn it out; you may need a converter.)
- Use common sense when it comes to sunbathing. Dermatologists recommend using

oil or lotion with at least a no. 8 SPF to protect your skin from the most harmful rays. You will still be able to get a nice tan, but you'll avoid a burn.

- You must bring documentary proof of citizenship, such as a certified copy of your birth certificate or an affidavit of birth and a photo ID such as a driver's license. Many countries will accept voter registration as proof of citizenship. A passport is always the safest assurance of reentry into the United States.

- You are allowed to bring up to $600 of duty-free goods back into the United States, except when traveling from the U.S. Virgin Islands, which has a limit of $1,200. Anything in excess of these amounts is subject to a duty fee of 10 percent. Keep all your receipts in your carry-on bag.

- Bring your cash in the form of U.S. traveler's checks, preferably in small denominations.

- Don't try snorkeling or scuba diving without instruction, available on most of the islands.

- The Caribbean islands offer so many activities that you can become exhausted if you try to do it all. There is no way to do it all, so pick and choose a few of the most alluring attractions, and plan time to be lazy, so you can relax and enjoy each other.

- English is at least one of the major languages spoken on most of the islands mentioned in this chapter, but in the Dominican Republic Spanish is the main language.

- It's always a good idea to ask your physician before visiting any of these islands.

You'll never be sorry if you decide to honeymoon in the Caribbean—it is a lovers' paradise. Have a perfect trip!

SEREN~ DIPITY HONEY~ MOONS

CHAPTER 25

BE A GOOD SPORT
Honeymoons for Outdoor Sports Nuts

Those of you who prefer indoor sports may think that "big game hunting" is using your remote control to find the Cal-Stanford football game on TV, but you will be amazed to learn that there are some newlyweds whose idea of a perfect honeymoon is to climb a mountain, catch a steelhead (that's a kind of fish, for all you couch potatoes), or snowshoe into the back country on a deer hunting trip. One honeymoon couple I interviewed had what they thought was an idyllic experience wilderness backpacking high above the timberline. They zipped two sleeping bags together and roughed it without a tent, beginning their married life communing with nature.

Another couple hitched a ride on a helicopter to a secluded Canadian lake where they spent a week fishing, camping, swimming, hiking, and enjoying the purity of the silence.

Whether you're nature lovers looking for an adventurous outdoor honeymoon, or a couple who just wants to enjoy a week of unlimited golf or tennis, your marriage will start out right on a wholesome sporting "high."

There are various ways to book one of these special honeymoons. You can plan your trip in à la carte fashion, making your own reservations for accommodations and all your sporting activities, or you can do it the easy way by making one reservation for an all-inclusive package plan. The best source of this information is the ads in specialty magazines that pertain to the sport of interest to you.

FISHING

If you both love to fish, whether deep-sea sport fishing, or stream or lake fishing, you will find cabins for rent, boats to charter and secluded private campsites, all advertised in the popular fishing magazines. Here are just a few of the magazines available for sale at your local full-service bookstore: *Outdoor Life, Flyfishing, Sport Fishing, Field and Stream, Sports Afield, Esquire Sportsmen, Fur-Fish-Game* and *Adventure West*.

These are only a few of the sporting magazines that offer information on places you can go for a romantic little fishing trip. There is nothing like fresh trout cooking over a campfire along a secluded stream, and because this type of outdoorsy honeymoon is so much less expensive than your more glamorous and glitzy choices, you can stay longer and have money left over.

Hunting

I was surprised to find so many couples where both the guy and gal are interested in this type of sport, but if this is your idea of a perfect honeymoon, then go for it! If it sounds fun to traipse through the wilderness, following animal tracks in the snow, then that is exactly what you should do. Here are a few magazines that have ads for hunting travel packages: *Adventure West, Wild West, Sports Afield, Bowhunter, Black Power Hunter, Deer Hunting, Big Game, Whitetail Strategies, Outdoor Life, Esquire Sportsman, Bow & Arrow Hunting* and *Fur-Fish-Game*.

Deep-Sea Diving

Here is another exciting and dangerous sport that makes for an adventurous honeymoon. You can hire a charter to go out into the deep, or you can just dive off the shore of your favorite clear-water beach. Here are a few magazines that have ads for diving destinations and package trips: *Scuba Times, Skin Diver* and *Sailing World*.

Other Adventure Sports

You know what kind of danger and adventure turns you on, whether it's bungee jumping, kayaking, parasailing, hot-air ballooning, hang gliding, skiing, snowmobiling, off-road motor-cycling or whitewater rafting. In any case, there is a magazine out there with appealing travel ads to help you with your planning.

If you don't want to plan your trip on an à la carte basis, you may want to consider what the national parks have to offer, discussed in chapter 28. National parks have many adventure activities available, along with lodging and facilities; in fact, they can be an answer for those couples who want to rough it, but not "too much."

Another way to enjoy nature and participate in sporting activities is to purchase an all-inclusive package at a dude ranch or guest ranch. Some are more "civilized" than others, but there are plenty to choose from, and I'm sure you can find one that is just right for your "outdoorsy needs."

Dude Ranches and Guest Ranches

Dude ranches and guest ranches come in a variety of styles, according to the interests of their guests, and these ranches may be the answer for you if you're interested in some or all of these activities: hunting, fishing, rodeo roping, gold mine exploring, rounding up cattle, back packing, whitewater rafting, cross-country or alpine skiing, wildlife tours, photographic safaris, canoeing, waterskiing, four-wheel driving, mountain biking, trap shooting, branding cattle, snowmobiling, tubing, fossil hunting, snowshoeing, heliskiing and ice skating.

An excellent source of information regarding these ranches is Gene Gilgore's *Ranch Vacations: The Complete Guide to Guest and Resort, Fly-Fishing, and Cross-Country Skiing Ranches*. This book has helpful one-page profiles on hundreds of ranches in the United States and Canada, including all the details on accommodations, seasons, activities, dining, entertainment and price ranges. In the back of the book you can find a ranch that exactly suits your interests and abilities. Contact individual ranches to see what their specialties are.

There is a wide selection of adults-only ranches that may be more fun for honeymooners.

In addition to Kilgore's book, you can also call the bureaus of tourism for each state that is of interest, or you can write or call one of the dude or guest ranch associations. These associations, along with all the bureaus of tourism are listed in the Resource section in the back of this book.

Sporting Honeymoons for the Slightly Less Adventurous

For all of you wimps out there, and I am one of them, too, you may be looking for a less dangerous outdoor sport, such as golf or tennis. If so, there are literally thousands of golf and tennis packages to choose from, complete with accommodations, one or more meals per day, evening entertainment, swimming pools, saunas, whirlpools, massages, driving ranges, videotaped private lessons in your sport of choice, golf carts, lighted tennis courts, and even a private beach on a lake or oceanfront.

Some packages have a wide range of prices. How much you pay may depend on whether golf or tennis is included as an add-on to a room charge, whether you provide your own meals, or whether you're at a four- or five-star destination resort where everything is included in one price. Let me give you a tiny sampling of a few possibilities around the country.

- PINE NEEDLES RESORT, Pinehurst, North Carolina
  Their Golf Lovers Golf Package includes lodging, three meals daily, unlimited golf, free use of all their recreational amenities, including a sauna, whirlpool, and free passes to the PGA World Golf Hall of Fame. Call (919)692-7111. Cost: Their rates are per person and vary according to the number of days and time of year:
  Summer Season, June 14-September 15
  7 day/6 night — $670 per person
  5 day/4 night — $455 per person
  3 day/2 night — $250 per person

Winter Season, November 22-March 13
7 day/6 night — $660 per person
5 day/4 night — $440 per person
3 day/2 night — $220 per person

Of course, your transportation costs to and from this resort are extra, but you can still hold your total expense to less than $1,500.

- WALT DISNEY WORLD RESORT, Lake Buena Vista, Florida
They offer a package golf deal that includes luxury accommodations at The Disney Inn, Disney's Village Resort, or the new Disney Vacation Club Resort, one round daily on any of five golf courses, breakfast daily, cart, club storage and cleaning, a bucket of range balls and 50 percent off admission to Disney's Pleasure Island. Call (407)827-7200. Cost: Starts at $150 per night, per person, depending on time of year.

- MAGGIE VALLEY RESORT, Maggie Valley, North Carolina
This resort offers packages that includes golf and tennis, golf cart, lodging, breakfast, dinner and nightly entertainment. Call (800)438-3861. Cost: Starts at $70 per night, per person.

This gives you a general idea of rates. Many golf and tennis resorts also have packages that include your airfare or a rental car. Your best source of information for these destination resorts are the ads in golf and tennis magazines, including *Golf, Golf Digest, Tennis* and *Tennis World*.

Other sources are your travel agent and the bureaus of tourism for the state or country in which you are interested. Again, that information is listed in the Resources section in the back of this book. Many of the hotels included in the various state honeymoons, along with those in Mexico, Canada and the Caribbean, offer optional golf or tennis packages. Be sure to ask when you arrange your accommodations; if they don't have a golf course on their grounds, there may be golf privileges at a course nearby.

If you decide on an outdoorsy honeymoon, I'm sure you'll leave any leftover wedding planning stress and worry back in the wilderness or on the golf course, and you'll return tan, relaxed, refreshed, and ready to take up your new roles of husband and wife back in the real world.

CHAPTER 26

GOTTA HAVE A HEART-SHAPED TUB
Couples-Only Honeymoon Destination Resorts

Now, 'fess up! You checked out the Table of Contents and skipped over the first twenty-five chapters so you could read about honeymoon resorts, right? As I researched this book I discovered that many couples' first choice is a resort that caters to honeymooners-only. Here's what these resorts say in their ads:

- Deep, heart-shaped whirlpool bath for two
- Your own sensual Swedish sauna, and shower-for-two
- Velvet-draped, king-size round bed
- Elegant glass-doored fireplace
- Cavort in your bubbly bath with your bubbly champagne
- Your own private swimming pool in your own private suite
- Your own private kingdom of pleasure
- Velvet-draped canopied bed with a golden crown overhead to inspire you
- Romantically lit dressing area
- Seductive Roman baths for two
- Slow dancing on your own private terrace
- Romantic fantasies take bloom amid lush surroundings

And this is only your honeymoon suite; now, add these free activities and entertainment:

Badminton	Hiking trails
Basketball	Horseback riding
Bicycling	Ice skating
Complete health club	Masseuse
Cross-country skiing	Miniature golf
Dancing to live music	Movies
Downhill skiing	Nightclubs
Driving range	Private lakes
Fishing	Putting greens
Full-course meals	Sailing
Golf	Sandy beach
Handball	Shopping
Heated swimming pools	Shuffleboard

Skeet and rifle ranges	Star-studded shows
Skibob	Tennis
Snowmobiling	Volleyball
Softball	Waterskiing

Well, you get the idea! If you're looking for a honeymoon setting "enveloped in sensuality," with "seductive meals" and plenty of stuff to do, a couples-only destination resort may be the answer. These resorts seem to be concentrated in the Pocono Mountains of Pennsylvania and various Caribbean Island locations, while others are scattered all over the country. Their all-inclusive rates are reasonable when you consider all the amenities. Here is information on a couple of these resorts, just to give you an idea of their rates. As the brochures say, these rates include everything, including meals, but they do not include airfare:

- MOUNT AIRY LODGE, Mount Pocono, Pennsylvania
  Call (800)441-4410.
  Per-couple rates:
  Per day: Starts at $120.
  6-day/5-night stay: Starts at $550.
  8-day/7-night stay: Starts at $735.
- THE SUMMIT COUPLES RESORT, Tannersville, Pennsylvania
  Call (800)233-8250.
  Per-couple rates:
  3-day/2-night stay: Starts at $289.
  4-day/3-night stay: Starts at $405.
  5-day/4-night stay: Starts at $505.
  6-day/5-night stay: Starts at $605.
  7-day/6-night stay: Starts at $705.
  8-day/7-night stay: Starts at $805.

Most honeymoon resorts also offer Airtour Package Rates that include airfare and airport transfers. Here is a typical rate structure for this all-inclusive Airtour package:

- CAESARS POCONO RESORTS, Lakeville, Pennsylvania
  Call (800)233-4141
  Per couple rates:
  3-night/4-day stay: Ranges from $1,123 from a Zone 6 city to $1,551 from a Zone 1 city.
  5-night/6-day stay: Ranges from $1,508 from a Zone 6 city to $1,903 from a Zone 1 city.
    Their Airtour packages are obviously more expensive from a Zone 1 city (West Coast) than from a Zone 6 city (from Ohio to the East Coast). Their Zone 2 through 5 cities are in between the West and East Coasts.

The nice thing about these Airtour Package rates is that they are truly all-inclusive. You will know ahead of time exactly what your honeymoon expense budget will be, much the same as with a cruise package. These resorts offer a lot for the money because they include so many indoor and outdoor activities, as well as meals and entertainment.

And the meals are anything but skimpy. Here is a typical day's menu for the Summit:

- BREAKFAST
  They will bring a full breakfast to your room or you can enjoy breakfast in their dining room, complete with breakfast dessert pastries.
- LUNCH
  A choice of fried chicken, tuna platter, corn beef sandwich, rigatoni with sausage, salad platter or Spanish omelette.
- DINNER
  Choose from New York sirloin steak, baked Virginia ham, trout stuffed with crab meat, fresh veal parmigiana, roast Long Island duckling or linguini with white clam sauce, all served with champagne.

If you would like to have a complete list of all the honeymoon destination resorts located in the Pocono Mountains of Pennsylvania, call (717)424-6050 (for immediate information) or (800)POCONOS (for free brochures). Or you can write them at:

Pocono Mountains Vacation Bureau, Inc.

1004 Main Street

Stroudsburg, PA 18360

The honeymoon resorts in the Caribbean are a little pricier than those in the United States, plus you will have the expense of airfare from Miami to your island destination. However, they are worth checking out.

How do you find out about all the honeymoon resorts available? There are several good ways. The best source of information is the advertising section in the back of the major brides' magazines. You will find dozens of ads for honeymoon destination resorts, along with their "800" numbers, offers of full-color brochures, and even demo video tapes.

Another source is your local travel agency; a third source is the bureau of tourism for each state or country of interest to you. These addresses and telephone numbers are listed under Resources in the back of this book. Unless you want to receive all kinds of general information, be sure to request specific information on honeymoon resorts.

If you decide to honeymoon at one of these exotic spots, enjoy your heart-shaped tub!

CHAPTER 27

ENTERTAIN US

Honeymoons in Exciting Cities

New York City, Chicago, New Orleans, Los Angeles and San Francisco

Some of you may have dreamed of honeymooning in London or Paris, or maybe even Tokyo, but your bank account doesn't match up with your dreams. So, why not fly or drive to one of our country's exciting cities instead? For those of you who long for some big-city vibes and superb entertainment, this chapter offers five possibilities: New York City, Chicago, New Orleans, San Francisco and Los Angeles. Every one of these cities has its own brand of goose bumps and can provide a dramatic, exciting honeymoon to remember.

NEW YORK CITY, MANHATTAN BOROUGH

If you've never been to New York City before, you're in for an awesome experience. It is an experience unlike anything you've had before, even if you've traveled in Europe, for nowhere in the world is there a more frantic place. Everyone is in a hurry. Horns are honking; cars are crashing into each other; people are waving their arms and swearing at each other. (Deep down in their hearts they are wonderful people, you understand.) New York City is called the Big Apple, and it's known as the entertainment capital of the world. But to me, its personality is like that of a wild boar that's been stung by a swarm of bees — and I love it!

There is so much to see and do in this town that you'll need several trips just to "do Manhattan," but if it's your first time, the one must-see is a Broadway play. I'll tell you later how to get discount tickets. Other musts are free or very affordable, so the big question is where to stay. I have a couple of suggestions listed below.

If you want your brand new marriage to last more than a week, *don't drive a car into Manhattan*. There are no exceptions to this advice. Driving your car into Manhattan and parking it is too expensive, and you'll be lucky not to have a mental breakdown on the way to the parking lot, wherever it may be. So, my advice is to use other modes of transportation; they are readily available, not that expensive, and *much* more fun! There are taxis, the subway, buses, trains, ferries, the Neighborhood Trolley, tour buses and charters, and, best of all — *shoes*. Yes, walking around Manhattan is pretty easy because it's flat, and you can see the city up close and personal — the only way!

Words of caution:

- Don't dress like a tourist; jeans and a well-worn T-shirt are the best. Keep your "touristy" camera hidden in an old daypack on your back, and keep your traveler's checks in a money belt or money sock. Try to blend in; don't draw attention to yourself.

- Don't use public transportation at night, other than taxis.
- Don't walk around town at night.
- Don't drive or walk through Central Park at night (it's considered safe during the day).

Now, for the fun stuff.

Free Attractions

- On your walking tours of Manhattan, be sure to see Chinatown, Greenwich Village (including Washington Square Park), the New York Stock Exchange building, the World Financial Center (composed of four major towers), the American Museum of Natural History, the AT&T Infoquest Center, Central Park, the Garment District, Grand Central Station, Park Avenue, Rockefeller Center, the major department stores (Abraham & Straus, Bloomingdale's, Lord and Taylor, Saks, and Macy's), The Market (a building at Citicorp Center with restaurants and shops), and all the other nooks and crannies of special interest to you. Before you leave on your honeymoon call ahead to the New York Convention and Visitors Bureau at (212)397-8222. They will send you general tourist information, including a map for your walking tours.

Low-Cost Attractions

- Take a ferry ride to the Statue of Liberty National Monument. Cost: $6.
- Central Park boating. Cost: $6 per hour.
- Empire State Building, Fifth Avenue and Thirty-Fourth Street, houses an observation tower. Cost: $3.50.
- Lincoln Center for the Performing Arts offers a one-hour guided tour. Cost: $7.50.
- Metropolitan Museum of Art, Fifth Avenue and Eighty-Second Street. Cost: $6.
- Museum of Modern Art, 11 West Fifty-Third Street. Cost: $7.
- Radio City Music Hall tour. Cost: $7.
- Take a Gray Line tour of the city. They offer 20 tours to the general public. Call (202)397-2620 for fares.
- Circle Line Cruises makes sightseeing easy and fun. They have several tours, including a three-hour, 35-minute trip around Manhattan Island and a Harbor Lights Cruise. Cost: $16.
- This is a "must-do": Take a ride on the Staten Island Ferry (leaves Battery Park once an hour). Cost: Round-trip fare—50 cents. (This is the biggest tourist bargain around.)
- Enjoy New York City's nightlife; the entertainment is unmatched anywhere in the world. You can find some spots where the entire evening will only cost the price of one drink, while other places charge a cover charge of $20 or so. Pick up a copy of *New York* or

The New Yorker magazines, or *The Village Voice* newspaper for all the current entertainment tips.

Affordable Midtown Manhattan Accommodations

- Days Inn, 440 W. 57th Street, has a rooftop swimming pool, room service, cable TV with HBO, plus a great little restaurant called The Greenery where you can grab a meal for about $20 for two. Call (800)231-0405. Cost: About $130 per night.
- Howard Johnson Hotel, 851 Eighth Avenue, has cable, plus "pay" movies, and a restaurant where your meal for two will run about $18. Call (212)581-4100. Cost: About $135 per night.

Special Splurges

- You must see at least one Broadway play, and here is how you can get same-day tickets for 50 percent off the regular price. Go to the TKTS booth at the corner of Broadway and Forty-Seventh Street between 3 and 8 P.M. See what's available for that night. The regular prices range from about $25 to $60, so you could get two great tickets for $60, if they are available. Try this idea on a weekday when they won't be as likely to be sold out. You may be able to afford a *couple* of plays if you get less expensive tickets.

CHICAGO

Compared to New York City, Chicago is tame, although known as the rough and tumble Windy City. Let's hope it's not too windy during your stay, for Chicago is really a wonderful place, bursting with interesting things to see and do.

Unlike Manhattan, you can drive your car into Chicago; just know ahead of time exactly where you're going and avoid rush-hour. A good map is a must. When you get where you're going, you won't be able to park on the street, but there are public and private parking garages available. The ideal would be to stay at a hotel that has an arrangement for guest parking. If you decide to park your car and leave it, or if you fly into the city, you will want to ride the El, the rapid transit line. The fare is only $1 during non-rush hours. To help make your stay memorable, call the Chicago Office of Tourism, (312)280-5740, for a free packet of helpful information.

Word of caution: It never hurts to follow some of the advice I gave earlier for touring Manhattan. In fact, use your head and be aware of your circumstances when visiting any big city, while honeymooning or not.

Free Attractions

- Start out your visit with a walking tour of the Pullman Historic District, a nineteenth-century model community. Start your tour from the Historic Pullman Center at 614 East

113th Street. (If you prefer a guided tour, the cost is $3.50.)

- Next, walk whenever you can to see Chicago's many interesting sites, including the Chicago Cultural Center, 78 East Washington Street; the Civic Center, 121 North LaSalle Street; Douglas Tomb State Historic Site, 636 East Thirty-Fifth Street; Garfield Park Conservatory in Garfield Park; Grant Park (on the lake between Randolph and Roosevelt), which has a yacht basin, gardens, and free concerts in the bandshell in the summer; Jackson Park (adjoins Burnham Park), where you can enjoy the beaches, play tennis or bicycle, or ice skate in the winter; Lincoln Park and Lincoln Park Zoo; the Merchandise Mart on Orleans Street (two floors open to the public); the Magnificent Mile (North Michigan Avenue), for shopping at fine stores and galleries; and the Petrillo Band Shell in Grant Park for free summer concerts.

Low-Cost Attractions

- Art Institute of Chicago, Michigan Avenue at Adams Street. Cost: $6.
- Field Museum of Natural History in Grant Park. Cost: $4.
- Museum of Science and Industry in Jackson Park, including the Henry Crown Space Center and Omnimax Theater. Cost: $5 for the museum and $5 for the theater.
- Sears Tower, 233 South Wacker Drive. Cost: $4.25.
- Take in a Cubs game at Wrigley Field, a Bulls game at Chicago Stadium, or a Bears game at Soldier Field. Also, the Black Hawks play at Chicago Stadium.
- Chicago is known for its fabulous nightlife, especially its jazz. Try Andy's, the Checkerboard Lounge, the Gold Star Sardine Bar and the Jazz Showcase. Sports bars are also popular, including the Cubby Bear Lounge, Ditka's, Harry Caray's, Nick's and Sports Market. If you like comedy, you must go to The Second City, where John Belushi and Nichols and May started out. At some of these spots the entire evening will cost the price of one drink, while at others the cover charge can run as high as $15 per person. Check out *Chicago*, a monthly magazine, and *Key — This Week in Chicago*, a free weekly magazine available in racks all around town.

Affordable Downtown Chicago Accommodations

- McCormick Center Hotel, Lake Shore Drive at Twenty-Third Street, is directly on the lakefront. You will have a wonderful view of the harbor and the city skyline from any room. There is a glass-domed swimming pool, a health club, a couple of nifty restaurants, and free transportation to the Magnificent Mile and entertainment. Call (800)621-6909. Cost: Starts at $129 for two.
- Quality Inn Downtown, 1 S. Halsted, offers cable TV, pay movies, a heated pool, and a very reasonable restaurant, plus entertainment. Call (312)829-5000. Cost: Rooms start at about $60 for two; entrees in the restaurant begin at $6.

Special Splurges

- Chicago has great theater; you can purchase same-day tickets at 50 percent off at the Hot Tix Booth, 24 South State Street (cash only).

NEW ORLEANS

Here is one of the most "foreign" cities in the country; if you're longing for a place that has no resemblance to "Mom and apple pie," this is it. It's a stirring of spooky narrow streets, a strange-sounding tongue, dark dens filled with music, French lace balconies, and incomparable dishes—oysters Bienville, filé gumbo, blackened redfish, and "dirty" rice and red beans. If you decide to honeymoon in New Orleans, be sure to stay in or near the French Quarter, the place to be. There you will find the infamous Bourbon Street, along with mule-drawn, fringed surreys, mysteriously shaded courtyards, and a wide range of street entertainers, including mimes, street musicians, jugglers and caricaturists.

Words of caution: Heed the same advice as given earlier for other city tours, but with this added note—don't visit the cemeteries unless you're on a guided tour. They're sometimes frequented by unsavory characters.

Free Attractions

- Take a walking tour of the French Quarter, the true heart of New Orleans. It is bounded by Canal Street, Rampart Street, Esplanade Avenue and the Mississippi River. The Quarter includes the Jean Lafitte National Historical Park, where you can join a free walking tour led by park rangers. Also, you must see Jackson Square, known as the city's Left Bank, where artists set up shop.
- Enjoy a free ferry ride from New Orleans to the West Bank; the ferry departs from the Canal Street and Jackson Avenue docks.

Low-Cost Attractions

- The Historic New Orleans Collection, 533 Royal Street in the French Quarter. Cost: $2.
- Hermann-Grima House, 820 St. Louis Street in the French Quarter. Cost: $4.
- Preservation Hall, 726 St. Peter Street in the French Quarter, is where traditional jazz began. Cost: $3.
- The Zoo, 6500 Magazine Street. Cost: $7.
- Take the Aquarium-Zoo Cruise. Cost: $6.
- Swamp Tour, departs from the Highway 51 bridge in Machac. Cost: $16.
- Take in a professional or college game, from the Saints to exciting action at Tulane and LSU. If you're honeymooning over New Year's Day, be sure to get tickets to the Sugar Bowl, played every year in the Superdome. Tickets can be ordered beginning the day after the previous year's Sugar Bowl by calling (505)525-8603. Cost: About $100 each.

- Enjoy New Orleans' nightlife for the price of a drink or small cover charge. Try Snug Harbor, 626 Frenchman Street, or Tyler's, 5234 Magazine Street, two of the best jazz clubs. Of course, Bourbon Street is the place to take in a variety of music, from traditional Dixieland to sophisticated nightclubs.

Affordable French Quarter Accommodations

- It's hard to believe, but you can actually reserve a room at Le Richelieu, a four-star hotel in the heart of the French Quarter, at a fairly resonable price. It has desirable amenities, including a lushly planted patio with a swimming pool, an intimate lounge and cafe, and, best of all, a safe place to park your car is included in the daily rate. Cost: $90 to $115 per night.

Special Splurges

- Enjoy a sternwheel steamboat ride on the *Natchez*, docked at the Toulouse Street Wharf. Their evening dinner/jazz cruise boards at 6 P.M. Cost: $32.50.
- You must have at least one meal at Antoine's, 713 St. Louis Street. You'll find it almost impossible to get reservations for dinner, but lunch presents few difficulties and will save you money, too. Cost: About $75 for two.
- Take a Cajun and Plantation Stories Excursion, a seven-hour tour to the San Franciso Plantation in Garyville. Departs from many hotels. Cost: $50.

LOS ANGELES

Los Angeles is the second largest city in the country, sprawling all over its 465 square miles. There are so many things to see and do that you will need to be selective when you plan ahead. Perhaps you will want to concentrate on three or four main things to see, such as a couple of live television shows, Disneyland, Knott's Berry Farm or Universal Studios.

Words of caution: Unless you're in Disneyland, or some other controlled location, don't be out at night; especially avoid Hollywood in the evening. Don't drive anywhere during rush hours, 6:30 to 9:30 A.M. and 3:30 to 6:30 P.M.

Free Attractions

- Driving tours and touristy side trips are very popular in the L.A. area, including famous Mulholland Drive, Malibu, Beverly Hills' homes, Rodeo Drive, Sunset Boulevard, Melrose Avenue, Santa Monica's amusement pier and Venice's boardwalk.
- Farmers Market, Third and Fairfax Avenue, is populated with cafes and shops selling food, clothing and gifts. You could easily spend two or three hours in this colorful market.
- Free tickets are available to dozens of television game shows, sitcoms and late-night

gabfests; however, you must pick them up on the actual day of taping. Check with the L.A. Visitors Information Centers at 695 South Figueroa Street or at 6541 Hollywood Boulevard.

Low-Cost Attractions

- Los Angeles Zoo, near the junction of Golden State and Ventura freeways. Cost: $6.
- A guided walking tour of historic downtown Los Angeles departs from the Bilmore Hotel's Olive Street entrance at 10 A.M. on Saturdays. Cost: $5.
- Enjoy L.A.'s nightlife, which ranges from discotheques with light shows, to comedy shops, dancing and musical entertainment. Try Culver's Club at the Pacifica Hotel, Fantasia at the Westin Bonaventure, or the Garden Pavilion in the Century Plaza. Read the entertainment sections of the local newspapers or pick up a copy of *Key, Los Angeles* for hundreds of ideas.
- The Universal Studios Hollywood tour is considered a "must-see." They are located at Lankershim Boulevard in Universal City. Cost: $26.
- Disneyland, 1313 Harbor Boulevard in Anaheim, is another "must-see." Cost: $27.50 per person, unless you stay at the Disneyland Hotel where two one-day passes are included in your hotel rate.
- Knott's Berry Farm, 8039 Beach Boulevard, Buena Park, is a nice extra. Cost: $21.95 for an unlimited-use ticket.

Affordable Los Angeles Accommodations

- The Pan Pacific Hotel, across the street from Disneyland at 1717 South West Street, Anaheim, has a special Magic Kingdom deal of $99 for the first night and 50 percent off each additional night. This rate is only available if you make advance reservations. Call (800)321-8976.
- The Millwood Inn in downtown Los Angeles is a restored historic bed-and-breakfast, a Queen Anne-style inn built in 1894. It is centrally located at 2653 South Hoover Street, with rates starting at $69 per night for two. Of course, this rate includes breakfast, which is a plus. Call (213)747-4300.

Special Splurges

- Take a sightseeing tour aboard a double-decker, open-top bus. See Hollywood landmarks and celebrities' homes. Call Hollywood Fantasy Tours at (800)782-7287. Cost: $40.
- Enjoy dinner at sunset at the Top of Five restaurant located on the thirty-second floor of the Westin Bonaventure Hotel. This restaurant specializes in broiled seafood, steaks, veal and pasta, as well as hot rock cooking at your table. There is entertainment, dancing and a panoramic view. Cost: About $80 for two.

SAN FRANCISCO

San Francisco is one of the most beautiful and memorable cities in the world. If you've never been to see her, you'll leave your heart, just like the song says. Unlike Los Angeles, San Francisco does not sprawl about, but stays tightly contained within its 47 square miles. This may give you the impression that it can be seen easily on foot, but with its steep hills, the city lends itself to cable cars and taxis. It is possible to walk from downtown to Fisherman's Wharf, and I've done it several times, but you'll need a nice, cool rest when you get there.

Words of caution: Go back and read the advice given for the New York City tour on pages 155-156. It is applicable to San Francisco as well.

Free Attractions

- Take a driving tour along the well-marked, 49-mile Scenic Drive through the city. Start at Civic Center and follow the blue, white and orange sea gull signs.
- Hang out at Fisherman's Wharf, a full day's worth of entertainment in itself, including Pier 39, street performers, Ghirardelli Square and the Cannery.
- Be sure to see Golden Gate Park (during the day), the site of Steinhart Aquarium, Morrison Planetarium, and the Japanese Tea Gardens.
- Take a walking tour through Chinatown (on the way from Union Square to Fisherman's Wharf, in case you feel like a healthy hike).
- Mission San Francisco De Asis at Sixteenth and Delores streets.
- Walk around North Beach, from Telegraph Hill down to the waterfront. It's noted for its art galleries, bookshops, international restaurants, and casual approach to life.

Low-Cost Attractions

- Ansel Adams Center, 250 Fourth Street. Cost: $4.
- Morrison Planetarium in Golden Gate Park. Cost: $2.50.
- DeYoung Memorial Museum on Teagarden Drive in Golden Gate Park. Cost: $5.
- The Japanese Tea Gardens in Golden Gate Park. Cost: $2.
- San Francisco Zoo, Sloat Boulevard and Forty-Fifth Avenue. Cost: $6.
- Coit Memorial Tower, Telegraph Hill (near the end of Lombard Street). This is a "must-see" because of the view. Cost: $3.
- Take in San Francisco's nightlife, including comedy clubs, musical entertainment and dancing at all the major hotels and famous spots such as the Great American Music Hall, Kimball's or Wolfgang's. Enjoy Irish coffee at The Buena Vista, 2765 Hyde Street, where the cable cars turn around.
- Of course, you'll want to take a couple of cable car rides; at under $10 per person, this is a "must-do" when you come to San Francisco.

- Call the San Francisco Convention and Visitors Bureau at (415)391-2001 and ask for all their free tourism information.

Affordable San Francisco Accommodations

- Howard Johnson Lodge at Fisherman's Wharf, 580 Beach Street. I have stayed at this hotel many times; I like its location and the adjacent restaurant, which is attractive and affordable. Cost: About $93 to $123 per night.
- Redwood Inn, 1530 Lombard Street, is reasonably priced with free parking, free continental breakfast, in-room coffee and free HBO. It is within walking distance to Fisherman's Wharf and the Golden Gate Bridge. Cost: About $60 to $75 per night.

Special Splurges

- Enjoy dinner at The Cityscape Restaurant located on top of the San Francisco Hilton, 333 O'Farrell Street. This is one of my favorite spots because of the view, cuisine and service. As the sun goes down, lights begin to sparkle around the city, from the Bay Bridge to the streets and buildings. It's a feeling that cannot be explained—you have to be there. Cost: About $80 for two.

CHAPTER 28

YOUR UNCLE SAMMIE HAS A SURPRISE FOR YOU

Affordable Honeymoons in National Parks

Did you know that your Uncle Sam has a secret honeymoon place preserved for you? Did you realize that national parks not only take your breath away with their grandeur, but offer affordable lodging as well? Here are seven of the best parks for your consideration; they were chosen because of their beauty, reasonable accommodations, and fun stuff to do. The suggested lodging is always within the "low" to "moderate" range, making it possible for you to have an entire week's honeymoon for about $750 or less. I'm assuming you want some kind of indoor lodging; however, if you want to rough it and stay in your own tent, a week's total expense can be as low as $300. There are plenty of beautiful national parks; don't limit yourself to those listed here. See the extensive list in the Resources section of this book for ideas.

BIG BEND NATIONAL PARK, TEXAS

Fun, Affordable Attractions

- Hiking:
  One day to Santa Elena Canyon.
  One day to Boquillas Canyon.
  A 5-mile round trip to Lost Mine Peak.
- Boating:
  Take a float trip down the Rio Grande on a rubber raft.
  Take a two-day raft trip, camping overnight on a sandbar, to Santa Elena Canyon.
  Take a one-day float trip to Mariscal Canyon.
- Photography:
  Early morning is best at Santa Elena Canyon.
- Birdwatching:
  Colima warblers.
  Peregrine falcons.
- Fishing:
  In nearby Black Gap Wildlife Management Area, a 20-mile stretch of the Rio Grande.
- Sightseeing:
  Fort Davis National Historic Site, a restored frontier fort.
  The ghost towns of Study Butte and Terlingua, along Highway 170.

Affordable Accommodations

- Chisos Mountains Lodge—Reserve a motel room or a stone cottage. Call (915)447-2291. Cost: About $65 per night.

Where to Write for Additional Information

- Superintendent, Big Bend National Park, TX 79834.

CRATER LAKE NATIONAL PARK, OREGON

Fun, Affordable Attractions

- Hiking:
  Discovery Point Trail.
  Garfield Peak Trail.
  Pumice Desert Trail.
  Castle Crest Wildflower Garden Trail.
- Bicycling:
  To Rim Drive from Cleetwood Cove.
- Photography:
  From Garfield Peak there is a clear view of Wizard Island, a small volcanic cone.
- Sightseeing:
  Nearby Cascade Mountains.
  Diamond Lake in Umpqua National Forest.
  Lake of the woods in Winema National Forest.

Affordable Accommodations

- Mazama Village, newer motel-type units. Call (503)594-2511.

Where to Write for Additional Information

- Superintendent, Crater Lake National Park, Box 7, Crater Lake, OR 97604.

GRAND CANYON NATIONAL PARK, ARIZONA

Fun, Affordable Attractions

- Hiking:
  There are many day hikes available, including South Kaibab and Bright Angel Trails.
- Whitewater adventure:
  Take a ride on a rubber raft or a wooden boat down the Colorado River.
- Muleback trip:
  Take a mule ride into the canyon on a one-day round-trip.

- Photography:
  Of course, the Grand Canyon is one of the most photographed spots in the world; try your skills.

Affordable Accommodations
- Grand Canyon Lodge, including cabins and motel units with magnificent canyon views. A dining room and cafeteria are part of the lodge, open only in the summer. Call (801)586-7686. Cost: About $50 per night.

Where to Write for Additional Information
- Superintendent, Grand Canyon National Park, Box 129, Grand Canyon, AZ 86023.

GRAND TETON NATIONAL PARK, WYOMING — YELLOWSTONE NATIONAL PARK, WYOMING, MONTANA AND IDAHO

Because Yellowstone is right up the road from the Grand Teton National Park, I have included them as one destination. You will find that Yellowstone is more primitive than Grand Teton, and you'll enjoy the contrast between the two parks.

Fun, Affordable Attractions
GRAND TETON NATIONAL PARK
- Hiking:
  There are half-day and all-day hikes, including a short "get acquainted hike" to Hidden Falls.
  There are also trails for experts only, such as the Leigh Canyon to Berry Creek wilderness trail, which is almost devoid of markings.
- Boat trips:
  On Jenny Lake and Jackson Lake, you can take a guided excursion or rent your own boat.
- Fishing:
  You can fish in any of the streams or lakes for cutthroat and native trout, using an artificial lure.
  Or, you can troll in Jackson and Jenny Lakes, using heavy tackle.
- Horseback riding:
  You can go on a guided ride or rent a horse for a day and take off on one of the high trails.
- Photography:
  One of the great sports in this park is shooting animals with your camera. You will definitely need a telephoto lens.

- Birdwatching:
Trumpeter swans, plus 100 other species of birds.
- Float trips:
Two-hour and four-hour rubber raft trips are available down the Snake River.
- Sightseeing:
The nearby historic town of Jackson.

YELLOWSTONE NATIONAL PARK
- Hiking:
Yellowstone has over 1,000 miles of well-marked, safe, hiking trails, including Storm Point Walk and Clear Lake Walk.
- Backpacking:
There are many excellent back country trails, including the Bechler Trail and Hellroaring Creek Trail.
- Horseback riding:
There are several excellent one-day guided trips from Mammoth Hot Springs Canyon. There are also longer trips that last a week or more.
- Boating and fishing:
The "in" place to fish is the Southeast Arm of Yellowstone Lake. You can rent a boat that can be hauled or towed from Bridge Bay to Plover Point, the gateway to South Arm.
- Photography:
The geysers are the most photographed sights and require a fast shutter speed.
- Birdwatching:
Trumpeter swan.
White pelican.
Gulls.
Double-crested cormorants.
Terns.
- Sightseeing:
Nearby Shoshone National Forest.
Conducted or package tours through Yellowstone Park.
A drive along Grand Loop, a 145-mile trip.

Affordable Accommodations
- Colter Bay Village, distinctive log cabins, originals built by pioneer settlers. Call (307)543-2811. Cost: About $65 per night.

Where to Write for Additional Information
- Superintendent, Grand Teton National Park, P.O. Box 170, Moose, WY 83012.
- Superintendent, Yellowstone National Park, P.O. Box 168, Yellowstone National Park, WY 82190.

ROCKY MOUNTAIN NATIONAL PARK, COLORADO

Fun, Affordable Attractions
- Hiking:
  There are over 300 miles of trail; some are designed for a half-day's walk, others are more strenuous climbs. The Visitors' Center has a booklet describing the various trails.
- Birdwatching:
  There are conducted bird walks, or you can enjoy watching on your own. June is considered the best month to see the largest variety of species.
- Bicycling:
  There are three routes open during the summer: Trail Ridge Road, Horseshoe Park/ Estes Park Loop, and Bear Lake Road.
- Fishing:
  The fishing regulations for this part of Colorado are special; you will need to obtain a copy.
- Sightseeing:
  Visit nearby Arapaho-Roosevelt National Forest and Lake Granby. A drive along Trail Ridge Road is a must; it takes you right over the top of the Continental Divide.

Affordable Accommodations
- Driftwood Lodge at Grand Lake overlooks Shadow Mountain Lake; it has a pool. Call (303)627-3654. Cost: About $65 per night.

Where to Write for Additional Information
- Superintendent, Rocky Mountain National Park, Estes Park, CO 80517-8397.

YOSEMITE NATIONAL PARK, CALIFORNIA

Fun, Affordable Attractions
- Backpacking on mule:
  There are various saddle trips available that will take you to Merced Lake and other high-mountain spots.

- Hiking:
  There are many trails, the most popular being The Loop. Use of these trails is regulated by the park ranger; you will need a permit.
- Fishing and boating:
  Dry fly-fishing is the thing to try along the Tuolumne and Merced rivers. Boating is allowed on a few of the lakes, but only without motors.
- Climbing:
  Yosemite National Park is one of the most popular for climbing; it is a dangerous sport and not for novices.
- Sightseeing:
  Yosemite Valley is a mile wide, flanked by granite walls, domes and peaks. You'll also want to see the groves of giant sequoias, especially those in Mariposa Grove. And don't forget that Yosemite Park is famous for its waterfalls, including Upper Yosemite Falls, Lower Yosemite Falls, Bridalveil Falls, and others. Nearby old gold mining communities, such as Amador City, Angels Camp and Columbia are worth a visit.

Affordable Accommodations

- Yosemite Lodge, near the foot of Yosemite Falls, offers a pool, sauna, whirlpool and fireplaces. Call (209)252-4848. Cost: About $50 per night.

Where to Write for Additional Information

- Superintendent, Box 577, Yosemite National Park, CA 95389.

If you would like to read more about these ten honeymoon destinations and the rest of the national parks as well, go to your library and look at a copy of *National Park Guide*, by Michael Frome.

One word of advice: If you think this type of honeymoon appeals to you, call and make your reservations *immediately*. As you can imagine, the lodging goes fast, so call and reserve a room as soon as possible, even a year or more in advance. You can always cancel your reservation later if you decide to go somewhere else, but it's almost impossible to book at the last minute.

Now It's All Up To You

CHAPTER 29

DECISIONS! DECISIONS!

Are you confused? Is your head swimming with honeymoon possibilities? Good! That's what I intended.

When you first picked up this book you may have thought you couldn't afford much of a honeymoon at all, but now you know you can have a fabulous honeymoon, even if your budget is meager. The challenge is deciding which of the plans is right for you.

One thing you may want to consider is combining two or three of the ideas. One honeymoon couple I interviewed wanted to go to Hawaii, but couldn't afford to stay there for very long, so they combined a five-day, four-night Honolulu stay with five days in Yosemite National Park. This gave them a honeymoon that included both the exotic and the great outdoors; they went to Hawaii first and then to Yosemite for a quieter setting after the colorful activity of Polynesia.

Another couple took a four-day, three-night Caribbean cruise and spent the rest of their time honeymooning in their own home state.

See how it works? You can be creative, too. You may end up spending one night in an exciting city, a few days in Mexico, and the rest of the time on a dude ranch. The choice is up to you.

Congratulations to you as you start your lives together as husband and wife. Whatever you choose, I know your honeymoon will be fabulous, romantic, and, best of all—*affordable*!

RESOURCES

Airlines

Aeromexico	(800)237-6639
Air Canada	(800)422-6232
Alaska Airlines	(800)426-0333
Aloha Airlines	(800)367-5250
America West	(800)247-5692
American Airlines	(800)433-7300
Braniff	(800)BRANIFF
Continental Airlines	(800)525-0280
Delta Airlines	(800)221-1212
Hawaiian Air	(800)367-5320
Mexicana	(800)531-7921
Midway	(800)621-5700
Northwest Airlines	(800)225-2525
Pan Am	(800)221-1111
Southwest	(800)531-5601
TWA	(800)221-2000
United Airlines	(800)241-6522
USAir	(800)428-4322

Bureaus of Tourism

ALABAMA
(800)252-2262 (out of state)
(800)392-8096 (in state)

ALASKA
(907)465-2012

ARIZONA
(602)542-8687

ARKANSAS
(800)643-8383 (out of state)
(800)482-8999 (in state)

CALIFORNIA
(800)862-2543

COLORADO
(800)433-2656

CONNECTICUT
(203)258-4290

DELAWARE
(800)441-8846 (out of state)
(302)736-4271 (in state)

DISTRICT OF COLUMBIA
(202)789-7000

FLORIDA
(904)487-1462

GEORGIA
(800)847-4842

HAWAII
(808)923-1811

IDAHO
(800)635-7820

ILLINOIS
(800)223-0121 (out of state)
(312)793-2094 (in state)

INDIANA
(800)289-6646 (out of state)
(317)232-8860 (in state)

IOWA
(800)345-4692

KANSAS
(913)296-2009

KENTUCKY
(800)225-8747

LOUISIANA
(800)633-5970

MAINE
(800)533-9595

MARYLAND
(800)543-1036

MASSACHUSETTS
(800)447-6277

MICHIGAN
(800)543-2937

MINNESOTA
(800)657-3700 (out of state)
(612)296-5029 (in state)

MISSISSIPPI
(800)647-2290

MISSOURI
(314)751-4133

MONTANA
(800)541-1447

NEBRASKA
(800)228-4307 (out of state)
(800)742-7595 (in state)

NEVADA
(800)638-2328

NEW HAMPSHIRE
(800)258-3608

NEW JERSEY
(800)537-7397

NEW MEXICO
(800)545-2040

NEW YORK
(800)225-5697

NORTH CAROLINA
(800)847-4862 (out of state)
(919)733-4171 (in state)

NORTH DAKOTA
(800)437-2077 (out of state)
(800)472-2100 (in state)

OHIO
(800)282-5393

OKLAHOMA
(800)652-6552

OREGON
(800)547-7842 (out of state)
(800)543-8838 (in state)

PENNSYLVANIA
(800)847-4872

RHODE ISLAND
(800)556-2484

SOUTH CAROLINA
(800)868-2492

SOUTH DAKOTA
(800)843-1930

TENNESSEE
(615)741-2158

TEXAS
(800)888-8839

UTAH
(801)538-1030

VERMONT
(802)828-3236

VIRGINIA
(800)847-4882

WASHINGTON
(800)544-1800

WEST VIRGINIA
(800)225-5982

WISCONSIN
(800)432-8747

WYOMING
(800)225-5996

Canadian Tourism Offices

THE NORTH

- Yukon Department of Tourism and Information

Bag 2745
Whitehorse, Yukon Territory
Y1A 5B9, Canada

- Northwest Territories Tourism Information
  TravelArctic, Government of Northwest
    Territories
  Yellowknife, Northwest Territory
  X1A 2L9, Canada

WESTERN CANADA

- Ministry of Tourism
  802 865 Hornby Street
  Vancouver, British Columbia
  V6Z 2G3, Canada
- Alberta Tourism
  10155 102nd Street
  Edmonton, Alberta
  T5J 4L6, Canada

MIDWEST CANADA

- Saskatchewan Tourism
  1919 Saskatchewan Drive
  Regina, Saskatchewan
  S4P 3V7, Canada
- Travel Manitoba
  155 Carlton Street, 7th Floor
  Winnepeg, Manitoba
  R3C 3H8, Canada

ONTARIO/QUEBEC

- Ontario Ministry of Tourism and Recreation
  77 Bloor Street W.
  Toronto, Ontario
  M7A 2R9, Canada
- Tourism Quebec
  800 Victoria Square
  Montreal, Quebec

H4Z 1C3, Canada

ATLANTIC CANADA

- Tourism New Brunswick
  P.O. Box 12345
  Fredericton, New Brunswick
  E3B 5C3, Canada
- Nova Scotia Department of Tourism
  P.O. Box 456
  Halifax, Nova Scotia
  B3J 2R5, Canada
- Prince Edward Island Visitor Services
  P.O. Box 940
  Charlottetown, Prince Edward Island
  C1A 7M5, Canada

Caribbean Islands Tourist Information Offices

ANGUILLA

- Anguilla Tourist Information Office
  271 Main Street
  Northport, NY 11768
  (800)553-4939

ANTIGUA

- Antigua and Barbuda Tourist Office
  610 Fifth Ave., Suite 311
  New York, NY 10020
  (212)541-4117

ARUBA

- Aruba Tourism Authority
  521 Fifth Ave., 12th Floor
  New York, NY 10175
  (212)246-3030

BAHAMAS

- Bahamas Tourist Office
  255 Alhambra Circle, Suite 425
  Coral Gables, FL 33134

(305)442-4867

BARBADOS

- Barbados Board of Tourism
  800 Second Ave.
  New York, NY 10017
  (212)986-6516

BERMUDA

- Bermuda Department of Tourism
  310 Madison Ave.
  New York, NY 10017
  (800)223-6106

CAYMAN ISLANDS

- Cayman Islands Department of Tourism
  250 Catalonia Ave., Suite 604
  Coral Gables, FL 33134
  (305)266-2300

CURACAO

- Curacao Tourist Board
  400 Madison Ave., Suite 311
  New York, NY 10017
  (212)751-8266

DOMINICA

- Caribbean Tourism Organization
  20 E. 46th St.
  New York, NY 10017
  (212)682-0435

DOMINICAN REPUBLIC

- Dominican Republic Tourist Office
  2355 Salzedo St., Suite 307
  Coral Gables, FL 33134
  (305)444-4592

GRENADA

- Grenada Board of Tourism
  820 Second Ave., Suite 900-D

New York, NY 10017
(212)687-9554

GUADELOUPE

- French West Indies Tourist Board
  610 Fifth Ave.
  New York, NY 10020
  (212)757-1125

JAMAICA

- Jamaica Tourist Board
  866 Second Ave.
  New York, NY 10017
  (800)223-5224

MARTINIQUE

- French West Indies Tourist Board
  610 Fifth Ave.
  New York, NY 10020
  (212)757-1125

MEXICO

- Mexican Tourist Information Office
  70 East Lake St., Suite 1413
  Chicago, IL 60601
  (312)565-2786

- Mexican Tourist Information Office
  2707 North Loop W., Suite 450
  Houston, TX 77008
  (713)880-5153

- Mexican Tourist Information Office
  10100 Santa Monica Blvd., Suite 224
  Los Angeles, CA 90067
  (213)203-8350

- Mexican Tourist Information Office
  405 Park Ave., Suite 1002
  New York, NY 10022
  (212)755-7662

PUERTO RICO
- Puerto Rico Tourism Company
  575 Fifth Ave.
  New York, NY 10017
  (800)223-6530

ST. MARTIN
- St. Martin Tourist Office
  275 Seventh Ave.
  New York, NY 10001
  (212)989-0000

TRINIDAD AND TOBAGO
- Trinidad and Tobago Tourist Board
  25 W. 43rd St., Suite 1508
  New York, NY 10036
  (800)232-0082

VIRGIN ISLANDS, BRITISH
- British Virgin Islands Tourist Board
  1686 Union St.
  San Francisco, CA 94123
  (800)232-7770

VIRGIN ISLANDS, U.S.
- U.S. Virgin Islands Division of Tourism
  343 S. Dearborn St., Suite 1003
  Chicago, IL 60604
  (312)461-0180

Car Rental Agencies

Alamo	(800)327-9633
Avis	(800)331-1212
Budget	(800)527-0700
Dollar Rent A Car	(800)800-4000
General	(800)327-7607
Hertz	(800)654-3131
National	(800)227-7368
Sears Car Rentals	(800)527-0770
Thrifty	(800)367-2277

Cruise-Only Travel Agencies

World Wide Cruises	(800)882-9000
or in Florida	(305)720-9000
Cruises, Inc.	(800)854-0500
Cruises of Distinction	(800)634-3445
Landry & Kling	(800)431-4007
The Cruise Line, Inc.	(800)777-0707
Cruise Collection, Inc.	(800)444-9060
The Travel Company	(800)367-6090

Dude and Guest Ranch Associations
- Colorado Dude and Guest Ranch Association
  P.O. Box 300
  Tabernash, CO 80478
- The Dude Ranchers' Association
  P.O. Box 471
  LaPorte, CO 80535
- Alberta Guest Ranch Association
  Box 6267
  Hinton, Alberta
  T7V 1X6 Canada
- British Columbia Guest Ranch Association
  P.O. Box 4501
  Williams Lake, British Columbia
  V2G 2V8 Canada

Home Exchange Clubs

Better Homes & Travel	(212)349-5340
Holiday Home Exchanges	(805)642-4879
Intervac	(415)435-3497
Teacher Swap (teachers only)	(516)744-6403
Vacation Exchange Club, Honolulu	(808)638-8747

Hotel Discount Companies

Entertainment Publications	(800)521-9640
Colonial Vacations	(800)548-2812
Encore Travel Club	(800)638-8976

Solid Gold	(604)688-2384
Concierge Card	(800)346-1022
Quest International	(509)248-7512
Privilege Card	(800)359-0066
"See America at 50% Discount"	
	(301)653-2616

Hotel Room Wholesalers

Concordia	(800)347-2659
Hotel Connections	(800)383-1969
Sunline Express	(800)877-2111

Hotels and Motels

Pay special attention to entries in this list that are marked with an asterisk (*). These offer good quality at affordable prices for budget-minded honeymooners.

*Allstar Inns	(805)687-3383
*America West Hotels	(800)547-4262
Best Western	(800)528-1234
*Choice Hotels (includes Comfort, Clarion, Rodeway and Quality Inns)	(800)221-2222
*Courtyard by Marriott	(800)321-2211
*Days Inns	(800)325-2525
*Fairfield Inn by Marriott	(800)638-8108
*Hampton Inns	(800)HAMPTON
Hilton	(800)445-8667
Holiday Inn	(800)HOLIDAY
*Howard Johnson	(800)654-2000
Hyatt	(800)228-9000
*La Quinta Inns	(800)531-5900
Marriott	(800)228-9290
*McIntosh Inns	(215)279-6000
Ramada Inn	(800)2RAMADA
*Red Carpet Inns	(800)251-1962
*Sundowner Hotels	(800)322-8029

*Susse Chalet	(800)258-1980
	(in NH: 800-572-1800)
Travelodge	(800)255-3050
*Vagabond Inns	(800)522-1555

National Parks

ALASKA

- Denali National Park
  P.O. Box 9
  McKinley Park Station, AK 99755
- Gates of the Arctic National Park
  P.O. Box 74680
  Fairbanks, AK 99707
- Glacier Bay National Park
  Bartlett Cove
  Gustavas, AK 99826
- Katmai National Park
  P.O. Box 7
  King Salmon, AK 99613
- Kenai Fjords National Park
  P.O. Box 1727
  Seward, AK 99664
- Kobuk Valley National Park
  P.O. Box 287
  Kotzebue, AK 99752
- Wrangell-St. Elias National Park
  P.O. Box 29
  Glennallen, AK 99588
- Lake Clark National Park
  P.O. Box 61
  Anchorage, AK 99513

ARIZONA

- Petrified Forest National Park
  AZ 86028
- Grand Canyon National Park
  P.O. Box 129
  Grand Canyon, AZ 86023

ARKANSAS

- Hot Springs National Park
  P.O. Box 1860
  Hot Springs, AR 71902

CALIFORNIA

- Channel Islands National Park
  1901 Spinnaker Drive
  Ventura, CA 93001
- Lassen Volcanic National Park
  Mineral, CA 96063
- Redwood National Park
  Drawer N
  Crescent City, CA 95531
- Sequoia and Kings Canyon National Park
  Three Rivers, CA 93271
- Yosemite National Park
  P.O. Box 577
  CA 95389

COLORADO

- Rocky Mountain National Park
  Estes Park, CO 80517
- Mesa Verde National Park
  CO 81330

FLORIDA

- Biscayne National Park
  P.O. Box 1369
  Homestead, FL 33030
- Everglades National Park
  P.O. Box 279
  Homestead, FL 33030

HAWAII

- Haleakala National Park
  P.O. Box 369
  Makawao, Maui, HI 96768
- Hawaii Volcanoes National Park
  HI 96718

KENTUCKY

- Mammoth Cave National Park
  Mammoth Cave, KY 42259

MICHIGAN

- Isle Royale National Park
  87 N. Ripley St.
  Houghton, MI 49931

NEW MEXICO

- Carlsbad Caverns National Park
  3225 National Parks Highway
  Carlsbad, NM 88220
- Guadalupe Mountains National Park
  3225 National Parks Highway
  Carlsbad, NM 88220

MAINE

- Acadia National Park
  P.O. Box 177
  Bar Harbor, ME 04609

MINNESOTA

- Voyageurs National Park
  U.S. 53
  International Falls, MN 56649

MONTANA

- Glacier National Park
  West Glacier, MT 59936

NEVADA

- Great Basin National Park
  Baker, NV 89311

NORTH DAKOTA

- Theodore Roosevelt National Park
  P.O. Box 7
  Medora, ND 58645

OREGON
- Crater Lake National Park
  P.O. Box 7
  Crater Lake, OR 97604

SOUTH DAKOTA
- Badlands National Park
  P.O. Box 6
  Interior, SD 57747
- Wind Cave National Park
  Hot Springs, SD 57747

TENNESSEE
- Great Smoky Mountains National Park
  Gatlinburg, TN 37738

TEXAS
- Big Bend National Park
  TX 79834

UTAH
- Arches National Park
  125 W. 200 South
  Moab, UT 84532
- Bryce Canyon National Park
  Bryce Canyon, UT 84717
- Canyonlands National Park
  446 South Main St.
  Moab, UT 84532

- Capitol Reef National Park
  Torrey, UT 84775
- Zion National Park
  Springdale, UT 84767

VIRGINIA
- Shenandoah National Park
  Luray, VA 22835

WASHINGTON
- Mt. Ranier National Park
  Tahoma Woods, Star Route
  Ashford, WA 98304
- North Cascades National Park
  800 State St.
  Sedro Wooley, WA 98284
- Olympic National Park
  600 East Park Ave.
  Port Angeles, WA 98362

WYOMING
- Grand Teton National Park
  P.O. Box 170
  Moose, WY 83012
- Yellowstone National Park
  WY 82190

INDEX

HAVE A BEAUTIFUL WEDDING...
Without Breaking the Bank!

Is there a wedding in your future? Or do you know someone who plans to tie the knot soon? Relax! *How to Have a Big Wedding on a Small Budget* tells you how to have it *all* — without mortgaging the house. Loaded with money-saving tricks and organizational tips, as well as lots of encouragement, this book provides hundreds of creative, innovative ideas that not only save money, but also make planning a wedding a fun, friend-and-family-involving process.

And... with the help of *The Big Wedding on a Small Budget Planner & Organizer*, planning your wedding will be easier. This comprehensive guide covers every aspect involved in planning a wedding, from the ceremony through the reception. Worksheets and charts thoroughly detail every conceivable expense, and the "things to remember" checklists help you stay on track and within budget.

Use this coupon to order now!